The Future Course
of U.S.-Japan
Economic Relations

DATE DUE

Brookings Dialogues on Public Policy

The presentations and discussions at Brookings conferences and seminars often deserve wide circulation as contributions to public understanding of issues of national importance. The Brookings Dialogues on Public Policy series is intended to make such statements and commentary available to a broad and general audience, usually in summary form. The series supplements the Institution's research publications by reflecting the contrasting, often lively, and sometimes conflicting views of elected and appointed government officials, other leaders in public and private life, and scholars. In keeping with their origin and purpose, the Dialogues are not subjected to the formal review procedures established for the Institution's research publications. Brookings publishes them in the belief that they are worthy of public consideration but does not assume responsibility for their accuracy or objectivity. And, as in all Brookings publications, the judgments, conclusions, and recommendations presented in the Dialogues should not be ascribed to the trustees, officers, or other staff members of the Brookings Institution.

The Future Course of U.S.-Japan Economic Relations

Papers by MASARU YOSHITOMI

RONALD I. McKINNON

JOHN C. DANFORTH

YOTARO KOBAYASHI

WILLIAM A. NISKANEN

MICHIYA MATSUKAWA

ANTHONY M. SOLOMON

HENRY D. OWEN

NOBUHIKO USHIBA

*presented at a conference at the Brookings Institution
on April 28, 1983*

Edited by EDWARD R. FRIED, PHILIP H. TREZISE,
and SHIGENOBU YOSHIDA

THE BROOKINGS INSTITUTION
Washington, D.C.

THE NATIONAL INSTITUTE
FOR RESEARCH ADVANCEMENT
Tokyo, Japan

About Brookings

THE BROOKINGS INSTITUTION is a private nonprofit organization devoted to research, education, and publication in economics, government, foreign policy, and the social sciences generally. Its principal purpose is to bring knowledge to bear on the current and emerging public policy problems facing the American people. In its research, Brookings functions as an independent analyst and critic, committed to publishing its findings for the information of the public. In its conferences and other activities, it serves as a bridge between scholarship and public policy, bringing new knowledge to the attention of decisionmakers and affording scholars a better insight into policy issues. Its activities are carried out through three research programs (Economic Studies, Governmental Studies, Foreign Policy Studies), an Advanced Study Program, a Publications Program, and a Social Science Computation Center.

The Institution was incorporated in 1927 to merge the Institute for Government Research, founded in 1916 as the first private organization devoted to public policy issues at the national level; the Institute of Economics, established in 1922 to study economic problems; and the Robert Brookings Graduate School of Economics and Government, organized in 1924 as a pioneering experiment in training for public service. The consolidated institution was named in honor of Robert Somers Brookings (1850–1932), a St. Louis businessman whose leadership shaped the earlier organization.

Brookings is financed largely by endowment and by the support of philanthropic foundations, corporations, and private individuals. Its funds are devoted to carrying out its own research and educational activities. It also undertakes some unclassified government contract studies, reserving the right to publish its findings.

A Board of Trustees is responsible for general supervision of the Institution, approval of fields of investigation, and safeguarding the independence of the Institution's work. The President is the chief administrative officer, responsible for formulating and coordinating policies, recommending projects, approving publications, and selecting the staff.

v

About NIRA

THE NATIONAL INSTITUTE FOR RESEARCH ADVANCEMENT was founded in 1974 through special legislation by the Japanese parliament as the result of initiatives by representatives from the government, business, labor, and academic communities. NIRA's central purpose is the advancement of interdisciplinary research that seeks solutions to the problems confronting modern society.

NIRA performs a number of functions. It conducts its own research, it delineates areas of research that are then commissioned to other research institutes, and it subsidizes research projects by private organizations. In addition, NIRA makes its facilities available to researchers, disseminates information, and provides opportunities for research training and education. NIRA maintains close contact with research institutions abroad in order to determine appropriate research subjects and to promote international joint research projects.

The guidelines for selecting research topics are endorsed by the Research Council, whose membership represents various sectors of Japanese society. Research is grouped under six program areas: food and population, energy, international relations, human environment, economic development, and urban and regional planning.

The results of NIRA's research are made public through lectures, symposia, and the distribution of printed reports. NIRA strives to promote effective use of its research results by combining several interrelated research topics into a single symposium and by arranging discussions between the researchers and those implementing the results of their research. NIRA also makes policy recommendations based on the findings of the research it conducts, commissions, or subsidizes.

NIRA's operating budget derives from contributions from the national and local governments and private sources. The president of NIRA is Atsushi Shimokobe.

Preface

JAPAN and the United States produce almost one-third of the world's goods and services, account for one-fifth of world trade, and are major suppliers of capital and technology to the developing countries. Therefore the manner in which the two countries manage their economic affairs, separately and together, is one of the principal influences on the world economy.

Japan–U.S. relations have been subject to recurrent strain, arising mainly from trade, which is not surprising in view of the amounts and kinds of goods exchanged. To view economic relations between the two countries primarily in terms of traded items, however, is too narrow a focus. In recent years financial, fiscal, and monetary policies in the two countries, through their influence on capital flows and exchange rates, have strongly affected both economies and the rest of the world.

The purpose of this conference, jointly sponsored by our two institutions, was to inquire into the Japan–U.S. relationship in this broad sense. Connections between trade and financial issues provide a useful framework for thinking about present and future problems between the two countries. The proceedings of this conference, summarized in this publication, are meant to contribute to this kind of approach.

We thank the panelists for their presentations and the distinguished present and former government officials, bankers, industrialists, and academic experts in the two countries who participated in the conference.

The Brookings Institution is grateful to the United States–Japan Foundation for providing funds to help support the conference and the publication of this report.

NAOTADA KURAKAKE
Executive Vice-President,
The National Institute
for Research Advancement

BRUCE K. MACLAURY
President,
The Brookings Institution

Acknowledgments

A NUMBER of staff members from the Brookings Institution and the National Institute for Research Advancement helped with preparations for this conference and publication. We are particularly grateful to Yutaka Harada and other staff members of NIRA for assistance in coordinating contributions of the Japanese participants in the conference and for related administrative work. We are similarly indebted to Julia Sternberg and Barbara Littell of the Brookings Advanced Study Program, who supervised the organizational arrangements for the conference; to Nancy Davidson, who prepared the manuscript for publication; and to Janet Smith, who was responsible for the typing.

EDWARD R. FRIED
PHILIP H. TREZISE
SHIGENOBU YOSHIDA

Contents

An Introductory Perspective

EDWARD R. FRIED AND PHILIP H. TREZISE

In Japan public concern over economic relations with the United States has long been widespread and intense. A reciprocal concern has developed in the United States as trade, investment, and financial links with Japan have grown, both absolutely and relative to economic ties to other countries. These mutual concerns are reflected in this volume of proceedings of a conference on American-Japanese economic relations jointly sponsored by the Brookings Institution and the National Institute for Research Advancement.

The main presentations and the discussions that followed them cover a number of specific subjects of shared current interest. These include the bilateral trade account, with its large Japanese surplus; the more particular trade problems that fall within the bilateral structure; the yen–dollar exchange rate; and the tendency for Japan to show a global surplus in its goods and services trade. A summary appears in the final section.

The thread connecting the different conference subjects is the enormous impact of each country's domestic macroeconomic policies on the two countries' mutual economic relations. Ten years ago this factor would have been scarcely noticed. Today it is close to being paramount, even though attention continues to be concentrated elsewhere. To introduce the conference discussion, we offer some comments related to this central point—more by way of emphasis than of summary.

Merchandise trade between the United States and Japan has reached very large proportions—nearly \$59 billion in calendar 1982, when both countries were operating below their economic potential. Japan's record surplus in this trade of almost \$17 billion[1] naturally has attracted much attention: it seems to confirm the existence of a competitive imbalance not only between individual sectors but between the two national economies themselves.

In itself, however, the figure is not especially meaningful, and

1. Calculated on an f.o.b. basis.

I

the emphasis given it is misplaced and even dangerous. The Japanese surplus in bilateral trade has been persistent but so have been American surpluses in goods trade with Western Europe and with the oil-importing developing countries taken as a group. These American surpluses normally will be overmatched by deficits with the oil exporters, Japan, and (in recent years) Canada. But since the United States has a very large surplus from the sale or lease of services and from income accruing from past investments and loans, the country's overall position in current international transactions has been in surplus as often as in deficit during the past dozen years.

Emphasis on bilateral accounts tends to imply that each country should seek to reach balance with each of its trading partners. But the gains from international trade are to be expected when countries sell those goods which they are relatively most proficient in producing. Under these conditions, balanced trade between two countries or even two regions would happen only by improbable accident. To impose bilateral balancing by political fiat would of course have the early and unwanted effect of reducing the volume of international trade by some very large fraction. In the end, this would be damaging not only to the two countries in question but to all countries.

As it happens, Japan's trade surplus with the United States is to a large degree structural. This does not make it any less of a political target, but it is hardly an economic distortion or even a surprise. The Japanese national import account is very heavily weighted with purchases of food, fuel, and raw materials. The United States, while a major supplier in this category, particularly of food, generally accounts for less than 15 percent of the total. Japan's exports are predominantly manufactures. By reason of income, the United States is the largest single country market for imports of manufactures, with Japan supplying one-fourth of the total. The result is a strong tendency toward surplus for Japan. This surplus will not soon disappear, and there is no economic reason why that should be expected or desired. Its actual size, however, has varied widely over the past decade, being significantly affected by various factors having little to do with underlying international competitive positions, notably the incidence of trade restrictions, the exchange rate, and levels of business activity in both nations.

As for restrictions, it is fair to say that Japan's participation in the postwar movement to liberalize international trade has been needlessly slow and grudging. Liberalization in Japan did not reach substantial proportions until the early 1970s, much later than elsewhere. And while conventional import restrictions, particularly customs tariffs, are now at quite low levels, the persistence of other restrictions—nontariff barriers—has been the basis for continuing and often acrimonious demands from the United States for more adequate market access.

Trade barriers have had an influence on the volume and on the composition of Japan's imports. That they have left a residue of mistrust abroad is also true. Recent measures taken by the government of Japan promise to remove many of the particular causes for complaint, but time will have to pass before Japan will be accepted as having a fully open market for imports.

The yen exchange rate has been another source of disquiet and misunderstanding. It is argued plausibly later in this volume that the yen has been undervalued in relation to the dollar so far as traded goods are concerned. If that is so, then Japan's export industries have had an unearned advantage over their American competitors. In this situation, the competitive difficulties of affected American firms are not imagined. They have unjustifiably lost sales and profits and their employees have lost jobs.

Not only the yen but other convertible currencies fell in value against the dollar in 1981 and 1982. Some, including the West German mark, fell further than the yen. A proximate although not the unique reason for this general phenomenon was the demand for dollar assets induced by differentially high interest rates in the United States and to a lesser extent by the purchase of dollar assets as a safe haven. It is perhaps more accurate to say that the dollar was unduly strong than to say that the yen or deutsche mark was unduly weak.

Nonetheless, the belief grew in some American business circles that the Japanese authorities had deliberately fostered a weak yen as a means of promoting exports. Actually, Japan moved in the opposite direction: intervention in exchange markets and restrictions on lending and investment abroad, all to support the yen's international value. This decision had political and economic rationales. For one thing, the benefits to export sectors from a depreciated yen were offset by the pain imposed on other sectors by costlier imports, most notably imports of petroleum. More generally, the yen's decline meant that Japan as a nation had to export relatively more real goods in order to buy any desired total of real imports. The losses in real income caused by this worsening in the terms of trade could not be ignored. Finally, Japan came under political pressure from most industrial countries to restrain its exports.

Other policies to strengthen the yen could have been tried. To be sure, the Japanese government's efforts to slow down outflows of funds had the immediate objective of relieving downward pressure on the yen rate. It may be countered that to have allowed capital to flow out without restraint would have pulled domestic interest rates up in due course and thereby strengthened the yen. In effect, greater dependence on market forces might have been the more effective exchange rate policy, but it would have required Japan's authorities to give up some control over monetary policy, which they were reluctant to do.

A strong argument can also be made that Japan should have pursued an easier fiscal policy—more public spending or lower taxes—along with a monetary policy aimed at raising interest rates. Japan in fact has had strong domestic advocates of this kind of policy mix. They were not able to overcome the prevailing worry about already high deficits in the national budget. (A political analogue, though in a different substantive context, is the resistance in the United States to higher taxes or reduced spending to bring down looming budget deficits. This would have permitted interest rates in the United States to fall sooner and further than they did and through the impact on capital flows would also have strengthened the yen against the dollar.) In any case, it should be clear that the policy choices open to Japan have been no easier than those in other countries. More to the present point, in Japan as in the United States, decisions on presumably domestic economic policy have a very large effect on economic relations between the two countries and on the international economic system in general.

Japan's global current-account surplus at times has been cited as a problem for the rest of the world. Since the subject is considered in detail at various points in this volume, the comment here can be brief. A tendency to generate a global net outflow of goods and services does appear to be a characteristic of Japan's affluent and high-saving society. It is not an inevitable outcome, however. Japan has large unmet needs at home—housing and public infrastructure are prime examples. These could readily absorb all its private savings if fiscal policy were sufficiently expansive.

At the same time, there is nothing reprehensible or undesirable about a persistent capital outflow from a leading industrial power.

Most of the world is chronically in need of more capital than can be provided from local savings. The flow of real goods and services from Japan is a contribution to world economic growth.

It is less certain that the financial side of the process has operated at optimum levels. Although Japanese financial institutions are extensive and highly developed, the capital market has still not been fully opened for foreign transactions. Nor has the flow of Japanese capital to developing countries—on both concessional and commercial terms—developed as rapidly as Japan's weight in the international economy would warrant. The result appears to have been to transfer part of the financing of capital outflows—and thus some of the risk—to banks and securities houses abroad. This has been the regular pattern for the high-income members of the Organization of Petroleum Exporting Countries (OPEC), which do not have the banking structure and expertise to lend or invest all of their surpluses on their own. For Japan it is less explicable.

In any case, the fundamental point remains. If for whatever reason investment demand at home does not lay claim to the full amount of Japan's savings and the excess spills over to other countries through a current-account surplus, the world stands to benefit. In a better-functioning world economy, most or all of the other advanced industrial countries would similarly be registering net transfers of capital—real goods and services—to the parts of the world where capital is scarce and brings higher economic rates of return.

It is helpful to draw back from the specific tensions in U.S.-Japan economic relations to see these two economies in a larger perspective. From a global point of view, they are the dominant economic actors. The United States stands not alone but well ahead. In world terms, Japan comes next, even though its GNP is exceeded by that of the USSR. For as a trader, an investor, a lender, and a technological innovator, this group of small islands has far greater influence on the course of the world economy than the Soviet Union or, by a wider margin still, Japan's other giant neighbor, China. By any meaningful economic measurement, bilateral problems between the two countries are submerged in importance by the combined effect of their separate economic policies on the world system as a whole.

During the rest of this century and beyond, the United States and Japan will be driven to seek ways to reinforce one another's economic capacities. It is clear that the seemingly most intractable bilateral problems have been more the consequence of unwisely disparate macroeconomic policies than of basic differences between two exceedingly productive national economies. The main task ahead is to discover how to achieve more nearly complementary policies within the limits set by advancing knowledge and, it must be hoped, rising levels of political sophistication.

The Framework
for U.S.-Japan
Economic Relations

An Analysis
of Current-Account Surpluses
in the Japanese Economy

MASARU YOSHITOMI

MY PURPOSE is to examine Japan's current-account surplus against the background of the postwar evolution of its balance of payments. In recent years, this current surplus has given rise to the criticism that Japan has consistently pursued a policy of export-led growth, with destabilizing consequences for the rest of the world. I believe the facts show a different picture. Japan has indeed become an international creditor, as befits the present level of its per capita income, the slowing of its rate of economic growth, and its unusually high rate of private savings. This suggests that Japan will continue to show a current surplus but one that is not likely to grow as a proportion of income. Nor should it be a problem for other countries. Indeed, the use abroad of some portion of Japan's savings should be a positive force in world economic development, as was the case for U.K. savings in the nineteenth century and for U.S. savings following World War II.

The evolution of Japan's balance of payments

From the end of World War II until 1957, Japan's merchandise trade account registered deficits in every year except 1950 (the outbreak of the Korean war). Beginning in 1958 the trade account showed surpluses, but for a number of years these surpluses did not exceed deficits in the service account. As a result, when domestic demand became strong at the prosperity phase of the business cycle, the balance of payments was placed under pressure, and the consequent decline in external reserves forced the authorities under the adjustable-peg system of exchange rates to tighten domestic management of the economy. It was not before the middle of the 1960s that the current account showed persistent surpluses, releasing the authorities from balance of payments constraints in their demand management. Reflecting such current-account surpluses, the long-term capital account since 1965 has shown a net outflow every year except 1980 (see table 1). However, receipts of investment income were continuously smaller than payments of such income until 1972, when the former surpassed the latter because of the rapid accumulation of private foreign

9

Table 1. *Summary of Japan's Balance of Payments, 1961–82*
Billions of U.S. dollars

| Year | Current account | | | Capital account | | Errors and omissions | Changes in external reserves |
| | Total account | Investment income | | Long-term capital | Short-term capital | | |
		Credits	Debits				
1961	− 1.0	*	0.1	*	0.6	*	0.3
1962	− 0.1	0.1	0.2	0.2	0.2	*	0.3
1963	− 0.8	0.1	0.2	0.5	0.3	*	*
1964	− 0.5	0.1	0.3	0.1	0.3	*	0.1
1965	0.9	0.2	0.4	− 0.4	− 0.4	*	0.1
1966	1.3	0.2	0.4	− 0.8	− 0.4	*	*
1967	− 0.2	0.3	0.5	− 0.8	0.5	*	*
1968	1.1	0.3	0.6	− 0.3	*	*	0.9
1969	2.1	0.5	0.8	− 0.2	− 1.5	0.1	0.6
1970	2.0	0.7	0.9	− 1.6	− 0.7	0.3	0.9
1971	5.8	1.0	1.0	− 1.1	5.5	0.5	10.8
1972	6.6	1.6	1.3	− 4.5	0.2	0.6	3.1
1973	− 0.1	2.7	2.2	− 9.8	2.4	− 2.6	− 6.1
1974	− 4.7	3.6	4.0	− 3.9	9.9	*	1.3
1975	− 0.7	3.6	3.9	− 0.3	0.8	− 0.6	− 0.7
1976	3.7	3.5	3.7	− 1.0	1.0	0.1	3.8
1977	10.9	3.7	3.6	− 3.2	− 2.2	0.7	6.2
1978	16.5	5.3	4.4	− 12.4	5.8	0.3	10.2
1979	− 8.8	9.0	7.0	− 12.6	6.4	2.3	− 12.7
1980	− 10.7	11.1	10.3	2.4	16.4	− 3.1	4.9
1981	4.8	15.8	16.5	− 9.7	7.6	0.5	3.2
1982	6.9	18.4	16.6	− 15.0	− 1.0	4.1	− 5.1

Source: The Bank of Japan, *Balance of Payments Monthly.*
* Negligible.

assets. The short-term borrowing required in the wake of the two oil crises temporarily reversed this trend.

Thus the Japanese economy has very quickly experienced several stages in the evolution of its balance of payments in the post–World War II period: first, an immature debtor country with current-account deficits (1945–64, Stage I); then a mature debtor country with current-account surpluses and net payments of investment income (1965–71, Stage II); and finally an immature creditor country with current-account surpluses, including net receipts of investment income (1972–present, Stage III).[1] In other

1. The balance of payments stage of an immature international creditor will be followed by the next stage of a mature international creditor, in which net receipts of investment income exceed deficits in the rest of the current account of goods and services exclusive of investment income, still resulting in a net outflow of capital. The terminology used to classify the balance of payments stages is borrowed from Nadav Harlevi, "An Empirical Test of the Balance of Payments Stage Hypotheses," *Journal of International Economics*, vol. 1 (February 1971), pp. 103–17.

words, in Stage I, the Japanese economy was an international borrower in both flow and stock terms; in Stage II, it became an international lender in flow terms; and in Stage III, it became an international creditor in both flow and stock terms.

These changes in the balance of payments largely coincided with stages in the development of exportable goods. During Stage I, Japanese exports consisted primarily of simple labor-intensive commodities, but with an increasing share of nonsophisticated electrical appliances and vessels. In 1959 such commodities accounted for nearly 60 percent of total exports. In Stage II, medium knowledge-intensive goods, such as sophisticated electrical appliances (color television sets and automobiles), and capital-intensive commodities dominated the Japanese export sector. In the early 1970s such commodities accounted for nearly two-thirds of the total value of merchandise exports. In Stage III, highly knowledge-intensive industries are becoming increasingly important; by 1980, they had already accounted for about one-third of total exports.

At the end of Stage I (1964), Japan became an Article 8 member of the International Monetary Fund (IMF) and became bound by the Organization for Economic Cooperation and Development (OECD) accord concerning the liberalization of capital movements. In Stage II, quantitative restrictions (quotas) on merchandise imports began to be liberalized and more emphasis was placed on the gradual decontrol of foreign direct investment in Japan. It was not until the middle of Stage III, however, that trade barriers in the form of tariffs and import quotas became among the lowest in the advanced countries. As Stage III proceeded, foreign direct investment in Japan as well as international portfolio investment by residents and nonresidents in Japan became substantially liberalized, with only a few exceptions. During Stage III, Japan became a major but young international creditor, making efforts at the same time to liberalize regulations on money and capital markets at home.

A question remains whether the present stage of Japan's balance of payments can be sustained, becoming comparable to that of the United States in the post–World War II period or to that of the United Kingdom before World War I. The answer to this question will depend on: (1) the tolerance of other advanced countries toward Japan's chronically large current-account surpluses; (2) the further liberalization of Japan's trade, financial, and foreign exchange markets; and (3) the extent to which the yen becomes an international currency.

The chronic current-account surplus

What determines the size of current-account imbalances and international capital flows?[2] The link between exchange rate movements and the current account is profoundly related to this question.

A commonly held assumption of perfect capital mobility holds that the larger the domestic savings, the larger the current-account surplus. Japan has had a high savings rate, thanks to about a 20 percent propensity to save out of disposable income and a relatively high share of corporate profit in national income. Nevertheless, there was a tendency toward current-account deficits up to the mid-1960s, as mentioned above. It was only after then that the current-account surplus became firmly established.

During 1965–72, under the adjustable-peg exchange rate system, the current-account surplus accounted for a rather stable share of nominal GNP—around 1.5 percent on average—except for the last phase of the Bretton Woods system, when the yen became unrealistically undervalued. Since the advent of the floating-rate regime, Japan's current account has registered both deficits and surpluses. This is, however, not so much attributable to exchange rate movements as to the two oil crises. Table 1 shows that in 1974–75 under OPEC I and also in 1979–80 under OPEC II the current account was in deficit. But the table also shows that in both the post–OPEC I period (1976–78) and the post–OPEC II period (1981 to date) consistent surpluses appeared in the current account. A total of the deficits and surpluses in the current account since 1973 shows that the cumulative current-account surpluses amounted to only 0.24 percent of GNP for 1973–82.

Not only domestic savings but also domestic investment and growth, together with exchange rate movements, are important in determining the size of the current-account imbalance. Further, the dramatic changes in the terms of trade caused by the two oil crises did not merely disturb the current account temporarily, but also created substantial differences in the current-account imbalance as expressed in nominal and real terms. In addition, OPEC shock–induced economic adjustments in the Japanese economy added to the surpluses in the current account.

Two questions should be posed regarding Japan's current-account imbalances. First, what explains the rather persistent

2. The literature on this issue is scanty. Insights are obtainable from Jeffrey D. Sachs, "Aspects of the Current Account Behavior of OECD Economies," Working Paper 859 (Cambridge, Mass.: National Bureau of Economic Research, 1982); and Sachs, "The Current Account and Macroeconomic Adjustment in the 1970s," *Brookings Papers on Economic Activity* 1:1981, pp. 201–68.

surplus of the current account, amounting to about 1.0 to 1.5 percent of GNP? The two oil shocks temporarily disturbed this pattern, but a return to the norm occurred within a few years after the outbreak of each oil crisis.

A persistent current-account surplus of this magnitude, however, does not necessarily indicate that the growth of the economy is export-led. A fairly constant current surplus of 1.0 to 1.5 percent of GNP means only that the absolute *level* of exports of goods and services persistently exceeds that of imports and that exports grow more or less in parallel with, not faster than, imports. Nevertheless, over the past ten years, the importance of the current surplus as a force for growth of the economy appears to have accelerated, and consequent trade frictions have grown more serious.

Thus, the second question, which I will discuss later, is: how can export-led growth and consequent trade frictions be consistent with the abnormally small cumulative surplus of the current account during 1973–82?

As to the persistence of the current-account surplus, two alternative explanations are available. First, unequal marginal productivities of capital can lead to current-account imbalances between countries. These imbalances would then be the result of differences in technology, industrial mix, or endowments of capital. Alternatively, different intertemporal consumption preferences, namely, savings behavior, can account for current-account imbalances between countries even when they have similar technologies. The former explanation tends to account for the underlying trend of Japan's chronic current-account surplus, whereas the latter may account for the resilience of Japan's current-account surplus in recovering from the large oil crisis–induced deficits.

If the first explanation is correct, that is, if different technologies or capital endowments are the main source of current-account imbalances, we might expect that high ratios of investment to GNP would be consistent with current-account deficits. Indeed, during 1952–67, total fixed capital formation (including private and public as well as residential construction) accounted for a rapidly increasing share of nominal GNP, growing from 20.4 percent to 32.5 percent. As mentioned earlier, most of this period registered a rather persistent deficit in the current account. From 1968 to 1973, total fixed capital formation as a share of GNP stopped rising, remaining stable at the high ratio of 33 to 36 percent. This change might be consistent with the emergence of current-account surpluses. Since 1974, a period characterized by the two oil crises and the floating exchange rate regime, the ratio of total fixed capital formation to GNP has declined to about 31 to 32 percent. Such a large decline in domestic investment ratios may be consistent with the rapid recovery of the current-account surplus from the two oil crises.

Of course, the relationship between investment ratios and current-account imbalances is not that straightforward. This is particularly so when strong governmental foreign exchange controls are exercised so that domestic policies to keep interest rates low will not lead to capital outflows. High domestic savings can then be bottled up to support high domestic investment ratios, rather than leaking abroad in the form of current-account surpluses.

In the absence of such capital controls, Japan's extremely high saving rates would likely have caused larger current-account surpluses, that is, larger capital outflows, during both Stage II and Stage III, in view of low interest rate policies at home. In Stage III, however, regulation of international capital movements was considerably relaxed and domestic interest rates were liberalized, particularly in secondary capital markets, which are more relevant to international portfolio investors than the primary market. The liberalization of secondary market interest rates has been hastened by the budgetary authorities' need to enable the primary market to absorb smoothly the massive issue of national bonds that took place in Stage III. The relatively small cumulative current-account surplus since 1974 should be attributed to the two external shocks and to greater domestic budget deficits rather than to regulation of international capital flows.

The current-account surplus can also be increasingly influenced by the rise in the endowment of capital. If the higher level of capital stock per worker reduces the rate of increase in real capital stock, the result can be an improvement in the current account. All other things being equal, international capital moves from highly capital-endowed economies to those that are less so. In fact, the growth rate of real capital stock in Japan declined from 10 to 15 percent a year during Stage II to 6 to 7 percent a year during Stage III—a decline that has been particularly evident from 1975 to date. The aforementioned development of highly knowledge-intensive industries also suggests that Japan is now in a position to transfer not only technology but also management know-how through capital outflows, particularly in the form of direct investment abroad.

In short, by progressing through stages in the evolution of its balance of payments in the postwar period, Japan has become a natural international creditor, helped by the slowdown of capital stock accumulation under largely unchanged savings behavior in the private household sector, and by industrial and managerial development from a labor-intensive to a highly knowledge-intensive economy.

This natural course of development did not occur smoothly. Instead, Japan has faced the strong resistance of foreign countries in accepting its persistent current-account surplus. This has been particularly so over the past ten years—the oil crisis era. I now turn to the question of why Japan's course in becoming an international creditor has faced such extraordinary resistance on the part of its trading partners.

Influence of the two oil shocks

It is rather surprising that over the past ten years the cumulative surplus of Japan's current account was only 0.24 percent of cumulative GNP at current prices. This ratio can be compared with 0.47 percent for West Germany and 0.11 percent for the United States during 1973–81. This ratio in Japan under floating exchange rates was also much smaller than the U.S. ratio of 0.70 percent during 1960–66 under the fixed exchange rate system.[3]

The question then arises as to why the Japanese economy is often perceived to rely heavily on rapid export expansion for its growth when the facts show that the cumulative current-account surplus registered since 1973 was relatively small. This perception became a particularly strong irritant to Japan's relations over the past ten years, when other industrial countries generally experienced slow growth and rising unemployment.

The concept of export-led growth, however, is too vague when used to identify problems generated in the world economy. Export-led growth can simply mean that exports are the driving force for economic expansion. In such a case, exports trigger domestic growth, which in turn stimulates strong demand for imports. As a result, exports may grow more or less in parallel with imports in the medium run (three to four years) as well as in the long run. This is the case for the high-growth period of the Japanese economy, say, between 1960 and 1970. In real terms (at 1970 prices, on a national-income basis), exports of goods and services expanded by 15.5 percent a year, a much higher rate than the 10.8 percent annual growth of real GNP, suggesting that Japan relied for growth largely on exports. However, imports

3. Figures for West Germany and the United States are taken from the 1983 *Economic Report of the President*, p. 65.

grew by 14.8 percent a year, registering a remarkably similar tempo to exports (see table 2). Thus if we call the growth pattern of Japan's economy during this period export-led simply because exports expanded much faster than overall demand, it might be equally characterized as "import-led," because imports of goods and services also expanded much faster than real GNP.

What really matters for the world economy, therefore, is not an expansion of exports as such, but a growth in the net export *surplus* of goods and services. The latter simply means that exports expand more rapidly than imports in real terms over an extended period of time. Such a growth pattern is undesirable because it could result in the export of unemployment to the rest of the world. Hence, a valid question to pose is whether Japan's economy could have been driven by export surplus–led growth in the past decade, when in fact its cumulative export surplus was a surprisingly small ratio of its cumulative GNP. Does this suggest that perceptions in the rest of the world of export-led growth in Japan do not accord with reality and result in unjustified criticism of Japan's growth pattern?

Unless there are major changes in the external terms of trade (export prices divided by import prices), the magnitude of the current-account imbalance should be the same in either nominal or real terms. The period since 1973 has witnessed unprecedented changes in the terms of trade due mainly to the two oil price shocks. This was particularly true for Japan because of its heavy

Table 2. *Japan's Current-Account Surplus and Growth in Gross National Product, 1960–70 and 1973–82*
Percent

Item	High-growth period (1960–70)		Oil crisis period (1973–82)	
	At 1970 prices	At current prices	At 1975 prices	At current prices
Net exports (average annual growth)	15.5	16.6	11.6	15.6
Net imports (average annual growth)	14.8	15.9	2.2	13.7
Gross national product (average annual growth)	10.8	16.4	4.0	10.2
Contribution of external surplus to cumulative growth of GNP	1.4	1.3	32.4	2.0
Change in terms of trade over period	6.2		−43.3	

Source: Economic Planning Agency, *Annual Report on National Income Statistics,* 1978, 1982.

reliance on imported crude oil and because of the oil crisis–induced sharp depreciation of its exchange rate.

In other words, Japan's surprisingly small cumulative external surplus after 1973 does not necessarily preclude the possibility of an expansion in the export surplus in real terms, given the sharp deterioration of Japan's terms of trade. That is in fact what happened between 1973 and 1982: exports in real terms (at 1975 prices) expanded by 11.6 percent a year in sharp contrast to a mere 2.2 percent annual growth in real imports. Real GNP increased by 4.0 percent a year during the same period. (These data appear in table 2.)

This represented an astonishing turnaround in the growth pattern of the Japanese economy. While exports and imports grew in parallel during the high-growth period of the 1960s, export surplus–led growth characterized the period after 1973. As noted, this is not reflected in the nominal trade figures; nominal exports grew at nearly the same pace as nominal imports after 1973 (by 15.6 percent and 13.7 percent a year, respectively). As a result, the expansion of the *nominal* external surplus (defined as an excess of exports over imports of goods and services at current prices) accounted for merely 2 percent of the increment of nominal GNP from 1973 to 1982. In sharp contrast, the expansion of the *real* external surplus contributed nearly one-third (32.4 percent) of the growth of real GNP during the same period. Measured at current prices, the economy registered little export-led growth. But measured at constant prices, extraordinary export surplus–led growth was realized.

As shown in table 2, a major difference between the high-growth era and the oil crisis era was in the movement of the terms of trade. From 1973 to 1982, Japan's terms of trade deteriorated by 43.3 percent, whereas they improved slightly during the 1960s. This deterioration was much larger than that in Germany and the United States, where the comparable figures were 7.4 percent and 24.5 percent, respectively. The real income loss in Japan due to the deterioration of the terms of trade amounted to 9.9 percent of real GNP in 1981. In other words, the worsening of the external current account caused by the deterioration of the terms of trade between 1972 and 1981 could be compensated for by exporting real goods and services to the extent of 9.9 percent of the 1981 GNP, as shown in table 3.

How and why did Japan compensate for the deteriorated terms of trade by exporting goods and services in excess of imports in

Table 3. *Real Income Loss in Japan during the Period Covering the Two Oil Crises, 1972–81*
Trillions of yen except as otherwise indicated

Item	1972	1981
1. Gross national product (at 1972 prices)[a]	92.3	135.6
2. Exports of goods and services (at 1972 prices)[a]	10.4	27.4
3. Imports of goods and services (at 1972 prices)[a]	8.2	14.5
4. Terms of trade (1972 = 100)[b]	100.0	51.0
5. Exports of goods and services (adjusted for terms of trade change)[c]	10.4	14.0
6. Real income loss[d]	0	13.4
7. Real income loss in proportion to gross national product (percent)[e]	0	9.9

Source: Economic Planning Agency, *Annual Report of National Income, 1983 Edition.*
a. Obtained by converting deflators at 1975 = 100 into those at 1972 = 100. Export and import figures include factor income.
b. Deflators for row 2 divided by deflators for row 3 and set at 1972 = 100.
c. Row 2 multiplied by row 4 (and divided by 100).
d. Row 2 minus row 5.
e. Row 6 divided by row 1.

real terms? In the first instance, consumers and business firms made the necessary adjustments to higher oil prices fairly quickly. Japanese firms and households perceived the two oil price explosions as permanent, that is, they assumed that the oil deficit in the current account could not be financed permanently by borrowing abroad. On a national-income basis, oil deficits appear in the form of excess expenditure over income on the part of both firms and households. For households, larger nominal consumption caused by the oil price increase would erode the propensity to save. On the other hand, if households saw high oil prices as permanent, they would have tried to restore the accustomed high saving rate instead of borrowing permanently to finance inflated oil-related expenses. To do that, they would have had to reduce nominal expenditures on items other than oil or energy.

In the case of firms, the established relationship between expenditures and corporate income is altered because of higher expenditures for petroleum. Consequently, the ratio of value added to gross value of product will decline sharply. To restore the previous relationship, instead of borrowing permanently, firms economized on fuel and reduced other costs. Thus, in the short run, after the outbreak of the oil crisis, domestic demand for goods and services other than oil declined in real terms, leading to higher savings in real terms. In other words, while both firms and households continued to maintain the pre–oil crisis level of real output (that is, real GDP), they spent less on nonoil goods in real terms. As a result, an export surplus in real terms could emerge, representing the difference between real GDP and real domestic demand.

What is the mechanism for realizing this external surplus? As described above, the absorption approach, reflecting changes in the spending behavior of both firms and households after each oil crisis, accounts for the availability of an exportable surplus. At the same time, the oil crisis–induced depreciation of the yen helped to switch production and demand from nontradable goods to tradable ones through favorable relative price changes for the latter against the former. Furthermore, tight monetary and fiscal policies, induced by both the oil crises and the currency depreciation, prevented imported oil inflation from being translated into domestic inflation. Such demand management also contributed to lower domestic absorption and consequently a higher export surplus.

Through this mechanism and the adjustments to oil deficits on the part of the major sectors in the economy, the underlying trend of a persistent current-account surplus reemerged after each oil crisis. However, maintaining the status of an international creditor despite the two oil crises has caused a considerable export-surplus expansion in real terms, resulting in the accusation that the Japanese economy is biased too heavily toward exports.

The medium-term sectoral investment-saving balance

A major feature of the Japanese economy in the 1970s was the sharp reduction in the growth rate of real GNP from about 10 percent during Stage II to about 4 percent during Stage III. As part of the change, the ratio of total fixed capital formation to GNP declined by about 4 percentage points between 1970–73 and 1978–81, a decline that was similar whether expressed in nominal or real terms. This decline was mainly caused by a large reduction in private expenditure on plant and equipment relative to GNP. During both 1970–73 and 1978–81, however, the level of actual GNP can be assumed to be close to potential (or high-employment) output. In each period, labor markets were in approximate equilibrium, with actual employment close to the natural level.

However, the sectoral investment-saving balance changed considerably between these two periods (see table 4).From 1970–73 to 1978–81 the excess of corporate investment over savings relative to GNP declined from 9.1 percent to 5.7 percent, while households' excess savings over investment remained essentially unchanged at 10.1 to 10.2 percent of GNP. As a result, the private sector as a whole (corporate and household) generated excess savings. In 1970–73 the general government budget (including the general account of both central and local government and the social security fund account) showed a small surplus. In 1978–81, by

Table 4. *Japan's Investment-Saving Imbalances, by Sector, 1970–73 and 1978–81*

Percent of nominal GNP

| Savings and investment | Sector | | | | | | | | Errors and omissions | |
| | Household | | Corporate | | Government | | Foreign[a] | | | |
	1970–73	1978–81	1970–73	1978–81	1970–73	1978–81	1970–73	1978–81	1970–73	1978–81
Savings (S)	15.8	18.9	16.3	10.4	6.8	2.6	...	...	...	...
Investment (I)	5.6	8.8	25.4	16.1	6.0	7.2	...	...	...	...
S – I	10.2	10.1	–9.1	–5.7	0.8	–4.6	–1.4	0.1	0.3	–0.1

Source: Economic Planning Agency, *Annual Report on National Account*, 1983.
a. Net flow.

sharp contrast, the deficit in the general government budget amounted to 4.6 percent of GNP. Roughly speaking, the decline in the ratio of private investment to GNP and the consequent rise in excess private savings in relation to GNP have been more or less offset by the increase in the ratio of budget deficit to GNP.

Despite the increased budgetary deficit during 1978–81, there was no indication of an acceleration of domestic inflation or of crowding out of private capital formation through higher real interest rates. Most of the excess private savings generated by the lower investment ratio were absorbed by the increase in the government deficit. Hence the excess private savings did not depress output, and noninflationary high employment was maintained. Nor did the decline in the private investment ratio generate an increase in the ratio of the current-account surplus to GNP. Thus the large government deficit has played two roles in recent years. One has been to keep the Japanese economy close to high-employment output by absorbing the excess private savings generated by lower private investment. The other has been to keep the current-account surplus in nominal terms approximately at the same ratio to GNP (about 1.5 percent) as in Stage II.

Implications for U.S.-Japan trade relations

Japan's chronic current-account surpluses imply that Japan will continue to incur large surpluses in its merchandise trade with the United States. This bilateral merchandise trade imbalance with the United States arises essentially from two aspects of Japan's balance of payments—the commodity composition of its merchandise trade and the chronic deficit in its services account.

Even if Japan's merchandise trade account were in balance, its large net imports of petroleum and other primary products would have to be offset by similarly large net exports of manufactured goods. Japan is endowed with few natural resources. In 1980, for instance, Japan's net imports of primary products amounted to 10.1 percent of GDP, as compared with U.S. net imports of primary products amounting to 1.9 percent. On the other hand, Japan's net exports of manufactured goods amounted to 9.1 percent of GDP, compared to only 0.5 percent for the United States. Japan's trade deficits in primary products are incurred not only in mineral fuels (6.7 percent of GDP in 1980) but also in crude materials (2.2 percent) and food, beverages, and tobacco (1.3 percent).

This unique structure of trade balances by commodity group tends to be reflected in Japan's trade balances by region (see table 5). Huge deficits in trade with the OPEC countries are offset by large surpluses in trade with the industrialized countries. Similarly, Japan incurs merchandise trade deficits with advanced primary commodity–exporting countries such as Canada, Australia, New Zealand, and South Africa. These deficits are offset by high surpluses in trade with the United States, the European Community, and the newly industrializing countries.

Japan's current account (see table 6) also shows large deficits in trade in services. These deficits are particularly notable in transportation, tourism, licensing, royalties, and management fees. This large deficit in services, as in the primary commodity trade, has to be financed by a surplus in manufactured exports. In this connection, Japan's trade surpluses with the United States tend to be amplified because Japan incurs relatively small service deficits

Table 5. *Japan's Balance of Payments by Region, 1981*
Billions of U.S. dollars

Component	World	United States	European Community
Current account	4.8	13.9	4.0
Trade account	20.0	16.3	10.8
Exports	149.5	38.7	3.4
Imports	129.6	22.4	7.3
Service account	−13.6	−2.2	−6.8
Credits	39.8	13.3	6.8
Debits	53.4	15.5	13.6
Transfers	−1.6	−0.2	−0.1
Long-term capital account	−6.4	−2.6	5.8
Changes in assets	−22.8	−4.1	−4.9
Changes in liabilities	16.4	1.5	10.6
Basic balance	−1.7	11.2	9.7

Source: The Bank of Japan, *Balance of Payments Monthly.*

Table 6. *Structure of Japan's Current Account, 1978–82*
Billions of U.S. dollars

| Year | Trade balance | Service balance | | | | | Unre-quited transfers | Current account |
		Trans-porta-tion	Travel	Invest-ment income	Other services	Total		
1978	24.6	−2.5	−3.2	0.9	−2.5	−7.4	−0.7	16.5
1979	1.8	−4.3	−4.3	2.0	−2.9	−9.5	−1.1	−8.7
1980	2.1	−4.3	−3.9	0.9	−3.9	−11.3	−1.5	−10.7
1981	20.0	−3.2	−3.9	−0.8	−5.8	−13.6	−1.6	4.8
1982	18.2	−3.5	−3.4	1.7	−4.8	−9.9	−1.4	6.9

Source: The Bank of Japan, *Balance of Payments Monthly.*

with the United States. This will continue to be true if Japan's net investment income continues to grow as a result of increased investments in the United States.

Conclusion

Since the mid-1970s Japan has become a natural and "immature" international creditor as part of the evolution of its balance of payments since the end of World War II. This progression to the position of international creditor has been accompanied by (1) a steady shift toward the production of products that are knowledge-intensive and have had a large proportion of their value added in manufacture; and (2) a reduction in the rate of increase of the capital stock in Japan. This creditor position, however, does not require an ever-growing current-account surplus. Instead, the likelihood is that export surpluses will amount to a rather stable proportion of GNP. Japan's new stage as an immature international creditor coincided with the oil crises era of 1973–81. To remain an international creditor, Japan expanded its export surpluses enormously in order to finance large oil deficits in the current account instead of borrowing permanently from abroad to finance such deficits.

This is why the current-account surplus at current prices remained only 0.6 percent and 0.8 percent of GNP in 1981 and 1982, respectively, while the expansion of external surpluses at constant prices fully compensated for the deterioration of the terms of trade, equivalent to more than 4 percent of GNP in each oil crisis. Unfortunately, this unique situation generated the perception that the Japanese economy always relies on export surplus–led growth—a perception that is not warranted by Japan's record during its high-growth period in the 1960s.

If a third oil crisis or another externally caused deterioration of the terms of trade against Japan can be avoided, its position of international creditor (chronic account surplus) may be more easily accepted by the rest of the world. The world economy still requires savings for economic development. Japan's financial and foreign exchange markets should be more fully liberalized to give the rest of the world easier access to Japan's savings. Indeed, mechanisms aimed at the active utilization of Japan's savings should be created instead of devising means of discouraging saving. It is, however, beyond the scope of this paper to explore the methods and institutional arrangements to promote direct and portfolio investment, including syndicated loans and concessionary foreign aid.

Financial Causes of Friction between Japan and the United States

RONALD I. McKINNON

NO ONE, I suppose, would quarrel with the statement that the economic relations between the United States and Japan do matter to their mutual prosperity. The world's two largest market economies cannot very usefully choose to divorce themselves from one another. It remains the case, however, that the relationship is marked by much misunderstanding in both countries.

A sizable example is to be found in the American view of Japan's trade and current-account surplus. That surplus is commonly considered to be unfair, unreasonable, and a sufficient justification for protectionist measures. But Japan will tend normally to have a surplus in its current international transactions, not through unfairness but because Japanese private savings currently outrun private investment requirements. That is, except during cyclical fluctuations or oil crises, total spending on private consumption, private investment, and government falls below total output. The difference shows up as net exports. This number would be considerably larger if the government were not incurring huge fiscal deficits that sop up the largest part of the excess private savings. For several years now, Japan's general government deficit has been on the order of 5 to 6 percent of GNP. Its external current surplus last year was under 1 percent of GNP.

A normal or chronic current surplus necessarily makes Japan an exporter of capital, a lender abroad, a natural international creditor. It has been less efficient in this role than as an exporter of goods. Japan's financial institutions and the Tokyo capital market can hardly be called undeveloped. Nonetheless, remaining controls on capital movements and certain officially determined institutional shortcomings continue to limit Japan's contribution to the functioning of the world's financial economy.

Considerable tension exists between this long-run desirability of liberalizing controls on capital movements and the short-run problem of an unduly weak yen caused by foreign overborrowing in Tokyo. This "overborrowing" results from the reluctance of Japanese officials to allow their interest rates to increase to international levels; and dollar interest rates are themselves too high primarily because of the huge U.S. fiscal deficit. The resulting *financial imbalance* between Japan and the United States is the principal cause of the economic and political frictions between the two countries at the present time. Mutual accusations of unfair trading practices are simply beside this main point. But the resulting protectionist measures could, unfortunately, be with us a long time, even if the financial imbalance is satisfactorily resolved.

With these general comments, which I think apply to the question of how Japanese-American relations will develop over the next decade, I wish to turn to a more immediate policy issue. This issue takes its overt form in the dollar-yen exchange rate. In 1981 and 1982 the dollar was misaligned against nearly all currencies, the most important being the yen and the German mark. Although the yen and the deutsche mark have appreciated moderately since November, the dollar is probably still substantially overvalued in relation to both currencies.

After an examination of the evidence for misalignment, I will go on to propose a concordance of central bank policies that would, I believe, not only bring substantial realignment of the external values of these principal currencies but would also help to promote the stronger and sounder recovery that the world so badly needs. But the international coordination of monetary policies cannot do the whole job as long as U.S. fiscal policy remains out of control.

The dollar, yen, and deutsche mark

In 1981–82, the U.S. dollar appreciated sharply in nominal terms against virtually all other currencies. The IMF's broad trade-weighted index of the dollar against the currencies of seventeen other industrial countries increased from 93.9, averaged over 1980, to 118.5, averaged over 1982. There have been huge devaluations by Mexico, Brazil, Venezuela, and Chile, whose "soft" currencies are not even in the IMF's exchange rate index. In 1983, although the yen has appreciated modestly, the dollar seems to be even stronger against European currencies.

But is the dollar overvalued in "real" terms? A full answer would require a detailed exchange rate, price, and cost comparison with all of the United States' trading partners. To simplify, ignore relationships with soft currencies of less developed countries, and also currencies like the French franc and Italian lira, which continue to depreciate to offset internal price inflation.

Focus instead on countries that are important world traders *and* have relatively stable domestic price and wage levels. At least in the short run, sharp changes in their dollar exchange rates are not likely to be offset by changes in their domestic prices. West Germany is the dominant hard-currency European country, around which countries including the Netherlands, Austria, Switzerland, Denmark, and Belgium form a bloc with very similar exchange rate and cost characteristics. In recent years, Japan has also shown better price-level stability than has the United States. (Britain is once more on the verge of becoming a hard-currency country, but its idiosyncratic exchange rate behavior in recent years is not analytically tractable.) Hence, the statistical problem reduces to one of comparing American international competitiveness to that of Germany (representing hard-currency Europe) and Japan.

My analysis of how to coordinate financial policies among the three countries will proceed in three parts. First, I shall establish rough purchasing-power parity relationships among these three major currencies by looking at *relative* domestic prices and labor costs. With average nominal yen-dollar and DM-dollar exchange rates in 1982 through April 1983, the dollar appears to be overvalued by approximately 15 to 20 percent. And this overvaluation generates protectionist pressure that threatens to undermine American support for free trade.

Second, from data on *absolute* price level and money growth in the three countries, what near-term monetary measures should be taken to help correct this dollar overvaluation? Because of the current worldwide depression, an appropriate strategy for realigning exchange rates in 1983 would be short-term monetary expansion in the United States, with only "normal" or below-trend monetary growth in Germany and Japan. So long as the dollar remains strong in the foreign exchanges, the monetarists' current criticism of the Federal Reserve System for allowing "excessive" U.S. monetary growth since October 1982 is unwarranted.

Third, the huge U.S. fiscal deficit magnifies dollar overvaluation and harms American manufacturing, mining, and agriculture. The resulting trade deficit accentuates protectionist pressures in the United States. Indeed, I shall demonstrate that the open U.S. economy may now be "anti-Keynesian": broad cuts in government expenditures and increases in (permanent) tax revenues are likely to increase output and employment.

Cumulative price inflation in the United States

The choice of a base year when foreign exchanges are thought to be in equilibrium is somewhat arbitrary, although necessary for tracing subsequent changes in the real exchange rate. In tables 1 and 2, 1975 is the base year. The nominal yen-dollar and DM-

Table 1. Estimates of the Real Exchange Rate: Japan and the United States, Selected Years, 1960–82

Index, 1975 = 100

Year	Yen-dollar rate Nominal (1)	Indexed (2)	Wholesale price indexes Japan (3)	U.S. (4)	Real exchange rate[a] (5)	Unit labor cost Japan (6)	U.S. (7)	Comparative costs[b] (8)	Real exchange rate[c] (9)	Wages in manufacturing Japan (10)	U.S. (11)	Comparative wages[d] (12)	Consumer price indexes Japan (13)	U.S. (14)
1960	359.9	121.3	56.1	54.3	117.4	41	70	0.59	207.1	13.6	47	0.29	33.2	55.0
1965	361.5	121.8	57.3	55.2	117.3	50	67	0.75	163.2	22.0	54	0.41	44.5	58.6
1970	358.2	120.7	63.8	63.1	119.4	52	79	0.69	183.4	43.7	70	0.62	58.0	72.1
1975	296.8	100.0	100.0	100.0	100.0	100	100	1.00	100.0	100.0	100	1.00	100.0	100.0
1976	296.6	99.9	105.0	104.6	99.5	100	102	0.99	100.2	112.3	108	1.04	109.3	105.8
1977	268.5	90.5	107.0	111.0	93.9	104	108	0.96	94.0	121.9	118	1.03	118.1	112.7
1978	210.4	70.9	104.2	119.7	81.4	102	114	0.90	79.2	129.1	128	1.01	122.6	121.2
1979	219.1	73.9	111.9	134.7	88.8	99	122	0.81	90.0	138.5	139	1.00	127.0	134.9
1980	226.8	76.4	131.7	153.6	89.1	100	137	0.73	104.7	148.8	151	0.99	137.2	153.1
1981	220.5	74.3	133.6	167.5	93.2	104	146	0.71	104.3	157.2	165	0.95	143.9	169.0
1982	249.1	83.9	136.0	171.1	105.5	108[e]	160	0.68	124.3	164.8	176	0.94	147.7	179.4
1982:														
Oct.	271.1	91.3	137.5	171.1	114.8	112	161	0.70	131.2	166.1	177	0.94	150.6	182.4
Nov.	265.1	89.3	137.2	171.8	111.8	110	161	0.68	130.7	166.4	179	0.94	149.0	182.1
Dec.	242.5	81.7	135.2	171.9	103.9	110	160	0.69	118.5	168.6	180	0.94	148.7	181.4

Notes appear below table 2.

Table 2. Estimates of the Real Exchange Rate: Germany and the United States, Selected Years, 1960–82

Index, 1975 = 100

Year	DM-dollar rate Nominal (1)	Indexed (2)	Wholesale price indexes Germany (3)	U.S. (4)	Real exchange rate[a] (5)	Unit labor cost Germany (6)	U.S. (7)	Comparative costs[b] (8)	Real exchange rate[c] (9)	Wages in manufacturing Germany (10)	U.S. (11)	Comparative wages[d] (12)	Consumer price indexes Germany (13)	U.S. (14)
1960	4.170	169.5	64.8	54.3	142.0	...	70	...	...	28	47	0.60	57.6	55.0
1965	3.994	162.4	69.1	55.2	129.7	59	67	0.88	184.4	43	54	0.80	65.9	58.6
1970	3.647	148.3	73.9	63.1	126.6	70	79	0.89	167.4	63	70	0.90	74.2	72.1
1975	2.460	100.0	100.0	100.0	100.0	100	100	1.00	100.0	100	100	1.00	100.0	100.0
1976	2.518	102.4	103.7	104.6	103.3	99	102	0.97	105.5	107	108	0.99	104.3	105.8
1977	2.332	94.4	106.3	111.0	98.4	102	108	0.94	100.0	115	118	0.98	108.1	112.7
1978	2.009	81.7	107.8	119.7	90.7	106	114	0.93	87.9	120	128	0.94	111.1	121.2
1979	1.833	74.5	113.0	134.7	88.8	108	122	0.89	83.5	127	139	0.91	115.6	134.9
1980	1.818	73.9	121.5	153.6	93.4	117	137	0.85	86.5	135	151	0.89	122.0	153.1
1981	2.260	91.9	130.9	167.5	117.6	122	146	0.84	110.0	143	165	0.87	129.2	169.0
1982	2.427	98.6	138.3	171.1	122.0	127	160	0.79	124.2	149	176	0.85	136.0	179.4
1982:														
Oct.	2.530	102.8	139.9	171.5	126.0	131	161	0.81	126.3	150	177	0.85	137.6	182.4
Nov.	2.555	103.9	139.8	171.8	127.7	131	161	0.81	127.6	150	179	0.84	138.0	182.1
Dec.	2.419	98.3	139.5	171.9	121.1	130	161	0.81	121.8	150	180	0.83	138.3	181.4

Sources: International Monetary Fund, *International Financial Statistics*, selected issues; Organization for Economic Cooperation and Development, *Main Economic Indicators*, selected issues.
a. Based on comparative changes in wholesale prices; column 2 divided by the ratio of column 3 to column 4.
b. Column 6 divided by column 7.
c. Based on comparative changes in unit labor costs; column 2 divided by column 8.
d. Column 10 divided by column 11.
e. Preliminary figure.

dollar exchange rates were fairly stable in 1975–76, interest rates were fairly well aligned, and rates of price inflation were moderate and quite similar across the three countries. After the breakdown of the Bretton Woods system of fixed exchange rates in 1971–73 and the first oil shock in 1973–74, relative price and cost relationships appeared to settle down in 1975–76.

Because many American officials believed then that the dollar was overvalued, 1975–76 is a conservative base from which to measure today's dollar overvaluation. In early 1977 the secretary of the treasury and other officials in the Carter administration began trying to talk the dollar down—particularly against the yen. In 1977–78 this exhortation interacted with a more expansive American monetary policy to reduce the dollar's value from about 290 yen in January 1977 to 190 in November 1978, when the U.S. government finally mounted a massive exchange stabilization program. A similar sharp fall of the dollar against the mark continued into 1979. The result was a substantial, but temporary, real undervaluation of the dollar in 1978–79.

Perhaps more important, high monetary expansion in the United States from 1977 to 1979—despite the sharp fall in the demand for dollars—touched off a much higher rate of inflation there. From 1975 to 1982, wholesale prices rose 71 percent in the United States, 36 percent in Japan, and 38 percent in Germany (see tables 1 and 2). Consumer price indexes show a similar divergence. Only in 1982–83 have the three countries converged to the same absolute rate of inflation—close to zero. But the cumulative impact of the higher American inflation since 1976 combined with the sharp appreciation of the dollar in 1981–82 have left both the yen and the mark undervalued.

Misalignment in U.S.-Japan manufacturing labor costs

No single price or cost index is likely to provide an adequate explanation of misalignment of real exchange rates, and some perspective on historical trends is important in judging the current value of any measure of the real exchange rate.

In comparing Japan to the United States, table 1 shows that pure price indexes alone don't reveal too much. With 1975 = 100, deflating the nominal yen-dollar exchange rate (column 2) with the ratio of Japanese to American wholesale prices yields one measure of the "real" exchange rate. From column 5, purchasing-power parity seems to have been reestablished at a level of approximately 100 in 1982. The net depreciation of the dollar from 297 yen in 1975 to about 235–240 in the first quarter of 1983 apparently just offsets the higher rate of inflation in the

U.S. wholesale price index. The use of consumer price indexes would yield a similar result.

Looking at labor costs, however, gives an entirely different impression. The OECD provides indexes of domestic unit labor costs of producing one real "unit" of manufacturing output. In table 1, column 6 shows an increase of 8 percent in Japanese unit labor costs since 1975, and column 7 shows an increase of 60 percent in the United States. Clearly, the nominal appreciation of the yen of about 20 percent since 1975 was insufficient to close this gap. The result is the 24.3 percent overvaluation of the dollar's real exchange rate averaged over 1982, as measured in column 9. In the first quarter of 1983, with the nominal exchange rate fluctuating between 230 and 240 yen per dollar, the real overvaluation of the dollar against the yen was between 15 percent and 20 percent by this alternative measure.*

However, the calculation of broad unit indexes of labor costs is inherently suspect because they contain dissimilar manufactured goods, which makes comparisons between countries even more difficult. What is needed is some supporting evidence of a fall in Japanese labor costs relative to American labor costs at existing exchange rates.

Table 1 shows the pattern of Japanese unit labor costs *rising* relative to those in the United States from 1960 to 1975. Starting from a much lower base, Japanese productivity growth in 1960–75 was much higher than that of the United States, but it was more than offset by more rapidly rising money wages in Japanese manufacturing. Columns 10 through 12 in table 1 show how, relative to the 1975 U.S. base, wages in Japan more than tripled from 1960 to 1975 compared with those in the United States. This rapid rise caused Japanese unit costs (column 8) to increase from 0.586 of American unit costs in 1960 to 1.000 in 1975.

Before 1975 this continual increase in comparative Japanese labor costs was consistent with real exchange-market equilibrium. Japanese manufacturing evolved from a limited range of simple goods toward increasingly sophisticated products. Low-technology goods, such as textiles and toys, were continually phased out as their unit labor costs rose. And output indexes tend to underweight quality improvements in high-technology goods. Continual increases in Japanese export prowess in new goods largely offset their increasing costs in old goods.

While productivity growth in Japan has been more modest

*Ed. Note: For a somewhat lower estimate of the undervaluation of the yen, see Niskanen's paper.

since 1975, it has remained considerably higher than in the United States, where it has been almost nil. And nobody could doubt that the Japanese capability of developing new export products is as great as ever. But since 1975 American money wages have grown more than Japanese—in sharp contrast to the record before 1975, as columns 10 to 12 of table 1 make clear. Column 9 shows, after exchange rate adjustment, the historically unusual fall in Japanese unit labor costs relative to their American counterparts from 1975 to 1982 *despite* the continual upgrading of Japanese industry from low-technology to high-technology products. The ultracompetitiveness of Japanese manufactured exports in American markets in 1982–83 is a manifestation of an undervalued yen.

Because Japanese wholesale prices increased more than Japanese unit labor costs in comparison with their American counterparts in 1982–83, the overvaluation of the dollar was manifested by a relative profit squeeze in American industry. Japan is a low-cost international producer because—despite the worldwide slump—industrial profit margins in Japan were better maintained than in the United States. And since 1975 Japanese wage restraint (relative to productivity growth) has been quite remarkable. However, a complete analysis of the relative profitability of Japanese and American industry is beyond the scope of this paper.

U.S.-German price level misalignment Since 1975 price inflation in the United States has been about 23 percent higher than in Germany, as shown in the wholesale or consumer price indexes listed in table 2. But following the March 1983 realignment of currencies within the European Monetary System (EMS), the DM-dollar exchange rate was about 2.5—hardly different from the 2.46 rate that prevailed in the 1975 base year. Consequently, the dollar appears overvalued against the mark by about 20 percent, using a real exchange rate calculation based on wholesale prices (column 5 of table 2).

Similarly, unit labor costs in German manufacturing rose less fast than in the United States—27 percent vis-à-vis 60 percent—because of higher German productivity growth and relatively restrained wage claims since 1975. The real DM-dollar rate based on unit labor costs (column 9) indicates that the dollar may be overvalued by about 24 percent, comparing the data for 1982 with the base year 1975.

Unlike in Japan, where apparent yen undervaluation is manifested in higher profit margins, in Germany the undervalued mark is manifested in prices of finished goods well below their American equivalents. Indeed, a profit squeeze and series of bankruptcies and industrial failures in Europe suggest that profit margins have not been as well maintained as in Japan. This lower European price level was accentuated in early 1983 by declines in both the French franc and British pound against the German mark.

European profit margins are now quite high in export activities that compete against American goods, although they remain quite low domestically. This undervaluation of European currencies as a bloc against the U.S. dollar (but not against the yen) will allow European industries to encroach on world markets for American tradable goods.

One important caveat to the above calculations should be noted. To some extent, apparent higher productivity growth of manufacturing labor in Europe since 1975 is illusory. Real wages have been pushed far too high to secure full employment. Thus the absorption of new labor into productive employment has been slower than in the United States. Moreover, the continual increase in European real wages leads firms to shed labor and thus apparently increases the productivity of those that remain because capital intensity per worker rises. This effect shows up as a relatively small increase in unit labor costs (table 2, column 6).

But this European method of achieving productivity growth is neither sustainable nor consistent with full employment. Thus the 24 percent undervaluation of the German mark against the dollar (column 9) is overstated. A figure of 15 to 20 percent is probably a better approximation.

In effect, Europeans have created heavy unemployment by allowing real wages to get too high. But each European country must solve this problem domestically. To lessen unemployment, it is unacceptable to use heavy export and production subsidies (which the Germans have not done) or the currency undervaluation that has happened more or less accidentally.

In paradoxical contrast to the European situation, international equilibrium probably requires some increase in real wages in Japan.

Adjusting the exchange rate through monetary policy

A strong case remains for official action to create better alignment of exchange rates. The yen and mark should both appreciate against the dollar by about 15 to 20 percent. But how should this be done? The exchange rate is merely a *relative* price. Either the United States or Germany and Japan—or all three—could adjust their financial policies to secure the desired change.

I would not advocate aggressive direct official intervention in the foreign exchange markets to correct the current disequilibrium.

Without supporting monetary changes, even massive intervention could be ineffective. On the other hand, any precipitate or discrete changes in current exchange rates would upset existing contractual relationships in international trade. Defensive intervention for exchange rate smoothing is, of course, warranted—particularly if aimed at preventing further dollar appreciation.

Instead, the focus should be on the basic sources of financial disequilibrium that led to an overvalued dollar. In 1981–83, for both political and economic reasons, the demand for dollar assets increased sharply at the expense of foreign-currency assets, of which those denominated in yen and marks were the most important.[1] Most of this ex ante increase in international demand was for nonmonetary interest-bearing dollar assets—such as U.S. Treasury securities, bank certificates of deposit, and industrial bonds. But this shift in international portfolio preferences had serious monetary consequences. The effective demand for dollar transactions balances and for the U.S. monetary base also increased sharply, as the demand for foreign central bank money fell.[2] In the United States, the depressive effect was that of unexpectedly tight money: unusually high real rates of interest and an overvalued currency that made American tradable goods less competitive on world markets.

A resolution suggests itself: German and Japanese money supplies should contract below their normal trend rates of growth, U.S. money growth should increase above its trend, or both. Which way to go depends entirely on the state of the international macroeconomy.

The current worldwide slump shows little sign of abating. In Japan the wholesale price index has actually fallen over the past year (February 1982 to February 1983). In Germany price inflation has abated, but unemployment is at an all-time high—above 8 percent. Over the past three years, cumulative monetary growth in Germany and Japan has been below its long-term trend. Clearly to call now for an appreciation of the mark and yen through monetary contraction in Germany and Japan is unwarranted.

However, American authorities don't seem to realize that a continuation of the worldwide slump may provoke the Bundesbank or Bank of Japan into a unilateral monetary expansion, the

1. In Ronald I. McKinnon, "How a Strong Dollar Threw the Fed," *New York Times,* January 23, 1983, these political and economic events are discussed in more detail.

2. How shifts in international portfolio preferences change the domestic demand for money is more fully worked in Ronald I. McKinnon, "Why Floating Exchange Rates Fail," June 1983, Stanford University.

initial impact of which would drive down the mark or yen even further in the foreign exchanges because financial markets are integrated on a worldwide basis. Paradoxically, foreign monetary expansion would accentuate the depression in American tradable-goods industries in the short run and would provoke even more virulent protectionism in the U.S. Congress. Unfortunately, there are signs that the Bundesbank may be stepping up German money growth and reducing its discount rate ahead of what the U.S. Federal Reserve System is doing. The Bank of Japan may be tempted to follow, leading of course to further yen undervaluation.

The only acceptable way out is for a sharp monetary expansion in the United States *not matched* by equivalent monetary expansions in Germany and Japan. Otherwise, if all three expand simultaneously, there is a long-run inflationary danger; and of course dollar overvaluation would not be corrected. The Bundesbank and Bank of Japan should agree to desist from any extraordinary monetary expansion. In return the Fed would agree to expand M1 or M2 above their long-term trends until the dollar comes down substantially in the foreign exchanges. And indeed, the Fed shows signs of trying to do just this. Since it temporarily suspended its M1 target in October 1982, the Fed has allowed U.S. money growth well above its long-term trend.

Because the overvalued dollar is a signal of unusually strong demand for money in the United States, extraordinary monetary expansion there is necessary to avoid depression. And as long as the dollar remains overvalued in the foreign exchanges with low monetary growth in Germany and Japan, the Fed need not fear development of undue inflationary pressures in the future. In the recent past when monetary expansion in the United States was "excessive," leading to subsequent upsurges in inflation, the dollar was very weak in the foreign exchange markets, inducing excessive monetary growth abroad.[3] Two such episodes of high money growth in the United States accompanied by downward pressure on the dollar in the foreign exchanges occurred in 1971–72 and 1977–79. The dollar is manifestly not weak at the present time, and monetary growth in foreign hard-currency countries has been below its norm for the past two or three years.

Another way of putting the matter is to note that the unusual increase in the international demand for dollars over 1981–83 contributed to the surprising fall in velocity of the U.S. monetary aggregates M1 and M2. There was a sharp upward trend in the

---

3. See Ronald I. McKinnon, "Currency Substitution and Instability in the World Dollar Standard," *American Economic Review*, vol. 72 (June 1982), pp. 320–33.

velocity of M1 in the 1970s until its sharp fall of 6.7 percent in 1982. The velocity of M2 fell 5.5 percent from 1981 to 1982. The continued unusually strong demand for dollars should cause further declines in the velocity of M1 and M2 in 1983. Extraordinary monetary expansion in the United States in 1983 is thus quite safe, from the point of view of long-run inflation, so long as the dollar remains strong in the foreign exchanges.

Of course, if the financial markets look only at the unusually high growth in U.S. monetary aggregates in late 1982 and early 1983, they may get needlessly upset, as did the Shadow Open Market Committee.[4] But the Fed could allay such fears by explaining that the overvalued dollar and foreign monetary growth are temporarily being used as indicators. Once equilibrium in the foreign exchanges is restored, the Fed will revert to more normal growth targets for domestic M1 and M2.

U.S. fiscal deficits and financial imbalance with Japan

As part of the quid pro quo for short-run monetary expansion and reduced interest rates in the United States, the Bank of Japan should stop suppressing interest rates in the Tokyo capital market. The yen became undervalued in 1981–82, in part because the Japanese government liberalized exchange controls on capital flows from 1978 through 1980, but then prevented domestic interest rates from rising to international levels. The result was foreign overborrowing in Tokyo: an outflow of private capital exceeded the Japanese trade surplus, resulting in an unduly weak yen. To prevent further yen weakness in early 1983, the Japanese government is trying to restrict banks from making yen loans to foreigners.

Because of its extraordinarily high rate of domestic saving, Japan, as has been noted earlier, is a natural creditor country. Rationalizing the international role of the Tokyo capital market is necessary for the long-run stability of the world financial system. Liberalizing exchange controls by 1980 was the first welcome step. Freeing Japanese interest rates is equally important to avoid periodic reversion to restrictions on foreign lending. And in early 1983, to correct the gross overvaluation of the dollar, a move to higher interest rates in Japan requires that the growth of

4. Shadow Open Market Committee, "Policy Statement and Position Papers," University of Rochester, March 6–7, 1983. Taking literally their recommendation of a 5.5 percent growth in M1 from fourth quarter 1982 to fourth quarter 1983 would call for virtually no growth in M1 for the remainder of 1983. Such a myopic tight money policy would, of course, cause a calamitous further appreciation of the dollar in the foreign exchanges.

money supply be severely limited. But the Japanese authorities understandably are reluctant to act alone, for they also have a recession to worry about. That is why a U.S. policy of relatively high money growth is so important at this stage. Otherwise, Japan and Germany may elect on their own to pursue easier monetary policies. The net result would be that the American recovery would be stunted and excessive slack in the world economy perpetuated.

But monetary policy, however well managed among the three countries, can't do the whole job. The sorry state of American public finances should be corrected. By appropriating almost all private saving, the federal budget deficit of over $200 billion severely injures American industry through high U.S. interest rates that crowd out productive investment. And the Japanese government is inhibited from relaxing interest rate ceilings in Tokyo, with the unfortunate consequences discussed above.

Massive dissaving by the federal government literally forces the American economy to rely on the savings of other nations. High rates of interest attract financial capital from Japan, Europe, and the third world, thus forcing greater appreciation of the dollar in the foreign exchanges. The resulting decline in American net exports merely reflects the trade deficit necessary to absorb capital from abroad. The U.S. trade deficit is thus caused and dominated by the much larger U.S. fiscal deficit.

Without the beneficence of a Japanese trade surplus and savings transfer to the United States, American real rates of interest would be even higher, making economic recovery more difficult. But the burden of absorbing this foreign capital falls disproportionately on American tradable-goods industries, which are understandably upset.

In short, for the United States to correct its trade deficit and prevent a severe outbreak of American protectionism, its fiscal house must be put in order. Surplus Japanese saving would then be freed to provide yen-denominated finance for the third world, a more appropriate role for Japan as a natural international creditor.

Is the American economy anti-Keynesian?

Conventional macroeconomic theory suggests that a depression is hardly the time to cut government expenditures and increase tax revenues. If the U.S. Treasury were to move strongly to reduce its fiscal deficit in 1983, shouldn't the authorities worry about a further fall in aggregate demand?

The opposite could be true. In 1983 U.S. GNP is likely to increase more rapidly with actual and prospective cuts in government expenditures or increases in tax revenues.[5] In this sense, the U.S. economy exhibits "anti-Keynesian" characteristics in 1983— although I don't claim that this anti-Keynesian situation holds at other times or for other countries.

My reasoning is already implicit in the analysis of the overvalued dollar and its monetary consequences abroad. However, it is useful to summarize the main points:

1. High actual U.S. fiscal deficits of the order of $200 billion absorb almost all American personal saving, increase real rates of interest, and crowd out productive investment.

2. Current fiscal deficits are the general public's best gauge of prospective future deficits. Thus an additional premium for future inflation, or some other form of future wealth taxation, is built into current long-term rates of interest.

3. High interest rates attract capital from abroad and cause the dollar to appreciate in real terms, thus depressing American tradable-goods industries. Because foreign capital can be actually absorbed only through a *cumulative* current-account deficit, the dollar initially tends to overshoot (appreciate more than its long-term real exchange rate would warrant). So too does the increased foreign demand for dollar assets initially fail to reduce American real rates of interest,[6] although ultimately they should fall somewhat if the trade deficit becomes big enough.

4. Finally, because of America's peculiar position at the center of the world dollar standard, a strong tendency for the dollar to appreciate induces governments of other hard-currency countries to contract their money growth rates.

The upshot is that these negative effects of U.S. fiscal deficits on aggregate demand may be greater than any short-run stimulus from increased defense expenditures or greater transfer payments to social security recipients. Curbing U.S. fiscal deficits in 1983, together with monetary harmonization to relieve dollar overvaluation, could therefore result in a *net* near-term expansion of the American economy.

Conclusion

Among financially open economies, the exchange rate indicates when national monetary policies are relatively too tight or too easy. The presently overvalued dollar is still sending a clear signal

---

5. Of course, high marginal tax rates are always counterproductive. Thus increased tax revenues should come mainly from a broadened tax base.

6. The failure of interest rates to adjust in the short run to a shift in international portfolio preferences is worked out more fully in McKinnon, "Why Floating Exchange Rates Fail."

to the American monetary authorities that they should ease up relative to their German and Japanese counterparts. Recent criticism of the Fed for unduly rapid monetary expansion in late 1982 and early 1983 is unwarranted.

Even with a more appropriate monetary policy, the large U.S. fiscal deficit would continue to depress the American economy. The real dollar exchange rate could not be fully realigned to restore American industrial competitiveness with that of the rest of the world. A large U.S. trade deficit and protectionist pressures in the U.S. Congress are the inevitable consequence—a foretaste of which has already been felt in steel, autos, motorcycles, and machine tools.

Nevertheless, there is scope for harmonizing the monetary policies of Germany, Japan, and the United States with great mutual benefit, even if the American fiscal problem is not satisfactorily resolved.[7]

7. A more comprehensive outline of how this might be done on a continuing basis is provided in Ronald I. McKinnon, "A Program for Monetary Stability," in Richard Levich, ed., *The Future of the International Monetary System* (New York University, forthcoming).

General Discussion

MICHIYA MATSUKAWA of the Nikko Research Center commented that the exchange rate in today's circumstances is influenced more by capital flows than by comparative changes in prices and productivity. This new situation has to be taken into account in exploring what might be done to bring about greater stability in exchange rates.

He also asked McKinnon how he would reconcile his suggestion that Japan increase its interest rates, as part of wider monetary coordination, with weak investment prospects in Japan. Real interest rates are already very high in Japan. To raise them would stifle investment and dampen economic growth, even in an environment that has been improved by declining oil prices. Furthermore, a decline in Japanese investment and economic growth would increase capital outflows and cause the yen to depreciate even more. The Bank of Japan would prefer to reduce interest rates, but in the interest of monetary cooperation it is holding them constant. Is not this the most one should expect?

McKinnon agreed that increasing interest rates would pose serious difficulties for Japan at the present time. Japan, like Germany, is in an exchange rate trap. To get out of their slump, both countries would like to reduce interest rates, but this would only increase the undervaluation of their currencies. That is why the United States is now the only independent actor in the system. Expanding its money supply now would be warranted by giving weight to international as well as domestic conditions. If it did so, as a quid pro quo Japan should stop managing interest rates in the Tokyo capital market. Japan cannot become a major international financial center and at the same time continue to manage its interest rates. These rates should be permitted to move toward the world level, but that level should be acceptable to Japan. Short-run monetary expansion in the United States at the present time would help to bring this about.

Fred Bergsten of the Institute for International Economics asked Yoshitomi two questions: (1) why had he made so little reference to the exchange rate in analyzing the evolution of Japan's balance of payments; and (2) would he agree, as McKinnon shows, that the liberalization of Japan's capital market contributed strongly to the undervaluation of the yen, and, if so, what should be done about it?

Yoshitomi responded that the depreciation of Japan's exchange rate after each of the two oil price shocks resulted in the yen's becoming undervalued, as he had noted in his presentation. Undervaluation of the yen, in turn, contributed to the expansion of the current-account surplus in real terms. After adjustment to each of the oil shocks was completed, however, the yen appreciated to a rate approaching equilibrium. For example, between early 1979, following the second oil price shock, and April 1980, the yen depreciated 45 percent against the dollar. By early 1981, however, it had appreciated by around 25 percent, recovering to a rate close to equilibrium. Then the combination of large fiscal deficits and high interest rates in the United States led to mounting unemployment, a strong dollar (a depreciating yen), and a deterioration in the U.S. trade account. This combination was bound to lead to serious trade problems. For that reason, he agreed with McKinnon that a change in the policy mix in the United States was necessary and had so urged in a letter published in the *New York Times* in February 1982.

In the context of these high interest rates in the United States, the timing of the liberalization of the yen (December 1980) did prove to be unfortunate. It encouraged the large net outflow of Japanese capital that caused the yen to depreciate, reversing its course following the completion of adjustment to the oil shock. It is true that the volume of Japan's exports fell in 1982, despite the depreciation of the yen, but that probably was the result of the world recession.

Robert Holland of the Committee for Economic Development asked McKinnon to elaborate on his thesis that an increase in the demand for dollars does not affect the prices of American financial assets, goods, or services.

McKinnon said a sharp increase in the demand for dollar assets and the resulting inflow of capital into the United States should bid down American interest rates and bid up interest rates abroad. This occurs, however, only if the exchange rate is fixed and the money supply is adjusted appropriately. Thus the capital inflow from Japan to the United States would have required monetary expansion in the United States and monetary contraction in Japan. Then this inflow into dollar assets would have bid down interest rates in the United States and bid them up in Japan. Such interest rate changes would tend to balance the international capital market and dampen the extent of the flows.

Without a stable exchange rate and coordinated monetary policies, however, the dollar overshoots in the foreign exchange market and U.S. interest rates are not bid down. Because of the overshooting of exchange rates, the correct interest rate adjustment does not occur; meanwhile, the American tradable-goods sector receives a devastating shock.

The dollar has to appreciate to the point where investors expect it is going to depreciate in the future. At that point, equilibrium is restored because foreign holders of dollar assets see a declining yield on holding dollars, taking into account the expected depreciation of the dollar.

Bunroku Yoshino, foreign policy adviser to the Keidanren, asked why high U.S. interest rates and the consequent overvaluation of the dollar did not stimulate economic recovery in Western Europe and Japan.

Yoshitomi said the situation posed two problems for Japan. An excessive expansion of Japan's exports would only lead to further protectionism in its markets, thus choking off this possible source of economic stimulus. Second, an undervalued yen limited the Bank of Japan's freedom of action to stimulate the economy through monetary policy. At present, Japan would prefer to reduce its interest rate to encourage domestic investment. It is constrained from doing so because the yen would then become more undervalued and trade problems would be worse.

McKinnon added that the question highlighted the existence of another paradox. A period of speculation in favor of the dollar, as from 1981 to the present, forces a net monetary contraction on the world economy. Other central banks intervene to defend their currencies. As a result, money growth in European countries and Japan has been unusually low for the past two or three years. Just the reverse occurs when there is an unexpected run on the dollar, as in 1977–78. Foreign central banks intervene massively to support the dollar, lose control of their money supply, and expand excessively. Thus, because of the way the world dollar standard works, speculation in the foreign exchange market determines whether the world is in a boom or bust. Coordination of monetary policy is necessary to prevent that from happening.

Lawrence Krause of the Brookings Institution asked McKinnon whether an undervalued exchange rate, which results from monetary policies and lasts for a few years, would not have real effects on the economy: for example, underinvestment in traded goods and services in the United States and overinvestment in Japan? If so, is not overshooting of the exchange rate in the opposite direction necessary to correct such structural effects? He also asked Yoshitomi why excess savings in Japan should not call for reductions in the favorable tax treatment accorded to savings in Japan. This would reduce savings, reduce the government deficit that is a concern in Japan, and avoid forcing the problem on the rest of the world.

McKinnon, in responding to the first question, said that capital markets are not as myopic as implied by the question. If equilibrium exchange rates are restored through the adoption of appropriate monetary and fiscal measures, and the situation looks to be sustainable, there will be no shortage of investment in American tradable-goods industries. Overshooting of the exchange rate in the opposite direction would not be necessary.

As to the second question, Yoshitomi said he was opposed to reducing tax incentives to save in Japan. In the short run, excessive savings are causing an excessively large government deficit, which now amounts to 5 to 6 percent of GNP. In fact, government outlays have grown from 22 percent to 34 percent of GNP in just ten years. The proportion in Japan is now equal to that in the United States. The Japanese government is trying to arrest this trend because it does not believe it should absorb savings by continual increases in the fiscal deficit.

In the long run, however, a high level of savings is needed in Japan because of the rapid aging of the Japanese population that is clearly in prospect. The labor force presently is comparatively young, with the ratio of workers to retirees about 7 to 1. In twenty years it will drop to 3.5 to 1, about the same ratio as in Europe and the United States. It would be imprudent to reduce incentives to save when a high level of savings will be necessary in the future to finance the growing burden of pensions and social security. It makes more sense to seek ways of using Japanese savings effectively for world development rather than to discourage such savings.

Trade Flows and Policies

The Politics of Trade

JOHN C. DANFORTH

I DON'T PRETEND to be an economist, an expert on exchange rates, or a student of Japan's culture and society. I claim to be an expert in only one thing, and that is politics. I'm a very good politician, and I think I am very much in tune with the political climate both in our country and as it is reflected in the Congress of the United States.

International trade is a political issue in our country. Trade policy is set by the Congress. Insofar as the administration determines trade policy, it does so under powers delegated to it by the Congress. The Congress, in turn, is sensitive, even overly sensitive, to the political climate.

By far the most important political concern of our constituents is jobs. It used to be inflation. Now it is clearly jobs.

I had an interesting experience last month back in my state of Missouri talking to people who during this period of economic decline have been participants in one kind of food program or another. I was attempting to talk to them about food programs. They didn't want to talk about food; they wanted to talk about jobs. Their view was that with jobs and the earnings from jobs they would be able to buy food.

So jobs is the key political issue of the day, and there is no doubt at all that in the minds of the people of this country their ability to find jobs and hold jobs is very closely related to international trade. Missouri has been a major producer of automobiles. We are now having something of a resurgence of automobile employment in our state. Under even the most optimistic outlook, however, employment in the industry is going to be well below the levels of, say, five years ago. A good part of this problem is that imports have taken over a very substantial share of our auto market—and people know that.

Politicians want to respond to the pressures they feel from their constituents, and we are feeling those pressures. While I think that there is still general philosophical commitment to free trade in the Congress of the United States, there is an increasing attentiveness to any seemingly plausible approach to keep out competing products. If free traders still hold sway in the Congress, it is certainly not by the margin of safety that existed just a few years ago.

The politicization of trade in the United States is a relatively new and growing phenomenon. In recent years, the small number of experienced Washington players in the executive branch and on the Hill who once dominated U.S. trade policy have been faced with growing pressure from forces less knowledgeable or less convinced by our traditional open trade philosophy.

Decline of the coalition for free trade

Just as constituent pressure has grown for relief from imports in an increasing number of sectors, so too have we seen the demise of America's free trade coalition. This loose coalition, made up of groups that joined in the past to champion free trade, once included organized labor. Many major industries, such as steel and autos, have also dropped out. And American agriculture—still the backbone of the coalition—has begun to question its free trade stand in the face of European export subsidies and ever-present Japanese quotas. All of this bodes ill for America's continued adherence to free-trade principles.

Last week I was managing a bill on the floor of the Senate, the so-called reciprocity bill. This legislation is really an antidote to rampant protectionism. An amendment was offered that would have given the courts the power to issue restraining orders and injunctions to keep out products from foreign countries on the ground that they were being subsidized or dumped on the American market. It would have been a clear violation of the codes of conduct worked out during the Tokyo round in 1979. But it would have provided instant relief from imports. A very intensive educational effort on the floor of the Senate was required to defeat it.

Of even more concern, there was at least a sign in that debate that trade policy is becoming partisan and that protectionism is seen as a way to win votes in elections to come.

In the past, the politics of trade was largely bipartisan. Members of Congress took stands based on the economic makeup of their particular constituencies. Similarly, one administration's trade policy was virtually indistinguishable from the next—firmly grounded in a liberal trade philosophy.

Congress recognized the political pitfalls involved in making day-to-day trade decisions and delegated administrative responsibility to the executive branch. Wherever possible, individual constituent trade problems were channeled into the network of trade procedures legislated by the Congress and administered by the executive.

All of this appears to be changing. Not only is trade gaining grass roots attention, along with the attention of the media, but it has already become an issue in the 1984 presidential campaign.

So that is the present state of affairs, which I think has to be recognized by all of us. The relationship between politics and trade policy certainly is something that is well understood in Japan. For example, it is well known that the United States has been trying to open up the Japanese market to some of our agricultural exports, such as beef, citrus, and tobacco, and that it has been very, very slow going. Why has it been slow going? Because the Liberal Democratic party has a solid base of support in the agricultural community in Japan, and the farmers have been applying political pressure against liberalization of imports. We have the same kind of situation here in the United States.

Growing danger of protectionism

Now, it is my view that if, as a matter of national policy, we were to succumb to extreme protectionism, there would be no real future for our economy. That is to say that protectionism means we concede that we cannot compete with other countries, that we cannot keep up with their innovations, with their improvements in productivity, with their research and development, and that we simply want to try to cling to what we have now. I believe that there is no future whatever in that.

A clear example of legislation that represents a certain surrender to protectionism is the domestic content auto bill. Passed by the House last year, this legislation is again picking up steam in the Ninety-eighth Congress. To me and to others who oppose it, the domestic content bill runs wholly counter to the need for improving our competitiveness. Yet last year it gained the cosponsorship of over half the members of the House and about twenty in the Senate.

If you look at the record of the Ninety-seventh Congress on trade, you will find over 250 substantive trade bills were introduced. I might add that of these almost 20 percent were focused directly or indirectly on Japan. In addition to the passage of domestic content legislation in the House, the Senate passed strict reciprocity language in a telecommunications bill. "Buy-American" provisions on steel were adopted as part of highway construction legislation. And President Reagan encountered his first veto override on legislation designed to protect American printers.

In view of the depressed state of the economy throughout the Ninety-seventh Congress, it is perhaps surprising that more protectionist legislation did not emerge. Nevertheless, a number of us were frequently called to the floor of the House or Senate to ward off the many attempts to include protectionist provisions in legislation otherwise unrelated to trade.

However, as politicians, we in the Congress of the United States, with the responsibility for trade policy, have to assure our constituents that there is some future for them, that they are going to have jobs, that they are going to be able to do something with their lives, that they are going to be able to earn a decent living. If you go to those people and say, "Well, we know you used to be an auto worker, you've lost your job, and you're never going to get your job back because our U.S. auto industry isn't going to be employing many people. But we've got good news for you. All you have to do is to go to graduate school at Cal Tech, master the art of designing software, and there will be a job for you," the average auto worker would give you the political equivalent of a blue slip.

We do have to recognize the effect of trade policy on jobs. Of course we cannot just live in the past. We must move into high-technology fields. We have to increase opportunities for service jobs. But it simply will not do for politicians to try to tell our people that there is no future to protectionism, and at the same time try to explain to them why in products where we are competitive we are unable to get into foreign markets.

How do we explain that in agriculture, for example, where we are competitive, we cannot export a number of our products to Japan? How do we explain that in telecommunications equipment—where we have a wonderful agreement that in principle provides access to the Japanese market—after two and a half years only a derisory $34 million of sales has been registered? How do we explain that it took a couple of years to gain access for a product as unthreatening as baseball bats?

Some people say, "The problem is Americans don't do things as well as the Japanese. We don't save as much. Our plants aren't as modern. Our workers don't work as hard. Japan is number one," and so on, and I guess that makes good reading. The problem is that it makes awful political speeches.

If you compare statistics on import penetration of competitive products between the United States and Japan, you cannot help but question the fairness of Japanese import practices. It is very difficult to explain why competitive American exports such as cigarettes, telecommunications equipment, oranges, or medical equipment have market shares in Japan ranging from only 1 to 7 percent whereas Japanese autos, steel, television sets, machine tools, and recording equipment have anywhere from 15 percent to 50 percent of the U.S. market.

The need for reciprocity

It is important that our country not take the route of protectionism. There is good reason for concern about the politicization of the trade issue and the partisan support for trade restrictions. But in order to ward off protectionism it is very important for us as politicians to be able to assure our people that they do have a fair chance to compete when we are competitive. I do not think that it is politically possible for us to take the position that our markets are going to be open while other markets are closed.

I believe that the approach taken in the reciprocity bill, which I have authored, is the right kind of approach: that is, to catalogue systematically those barriers that exist to U.S. exports and to work at getting them taken down.

The legislation builds on the broad concept of reciprocity of market access that is fundamental to U.S. trade policy. It strengthens enforcement of the legal rights of the United States under existing trade agreements and it sets the stage for the expansion of those international rights through the negotiation of agreements in the service and investment areas. Finally, the bill addresses itself to the problems encountered by high-technology industries when government intervention has the effect of distorting international trade in these high-growth sectors.

Overall, the bill is designed to liberalize international trade and to curb protectionist pressures in the United States by demonstrating that we will enforce our rights under international agreements. The idea is to close the credibility gap created when we consistently refuse to take protectionist actions in spite of the widespread perception that we are the only country practicing what everyone else preaches—namely, free trade.

Specifically, the bill provides for:

1. A systematic procedure whereby the administration would identify and analyze key barriers to U.S. trade in products, services, and investment. The required annual report to Congress would include major foreign barriers to U.S. exports of products (including agricultural commodities), services, and investment. It would provide estimates of their impact on the U.S. economy

and it would describe efforts to achieve their elimination. It is my expectation, and that of others involved in the evolution of this bill, that these national trade estimates will be used by this and subsequent administrations to identify the most onerous barriers to U.S. trade and investment and thereby to set comprehensive market enhancement priorities for U.S. trade policy.

2. Section 301 of the Trade Act of 1974 would be amended to broaden its scope and to clarify and enhance presidential authority to retaliate against foreign unfair trade practices. In this regard, the range of unfair trade practices for which relief is available under U.S. law would be broadened to cover performance requirements and other trade-distorting barriers to investment, as well as violations of intellectual property rights.

Foreign barriers not removed through negotiation or enforcement of the General Agreement on Tariffs and Trade (GATT) could be offset by the United States through the withdrawal of prior U.S. concessions or by the imposition of duties and other restrictions available under present law as clarified by this legislation. Of particular interest is the clarification of the president's authority to impose fees and restrictions on foreign services or suppliers of those services. While the role of regulatory agencies is recognized with respect to trade in services, I am firmly convinced that the Congress never intended regulatory agencies to make trade policy.

Where U.S. retaliatory options are not currently available to the president, he would be given new authority to propose legislation that would enjoy accelerated consideration by the Congress.

3. Finally, the legislation provides for major negotiations to achieve international agreements that encourage fair and open trade in services, investment flows, and high technology.

The reciprocity bill says that the United States is going to have to be as free to compete in foreign markets as people in other countries are to compete in the U.S. market. I believe that Japan, which now has a surplus of almost $20 billion with the United States in trade, must recognize that a situation that is all give and no take is one that ultimately is as unhealthy for the Japanese people as it is for us.

Many of the economic problems facing the United States today will not go away any time soon. They will not go away with the next election. Long-term structural changes and the need for adjustment have been exacerbated, not created, by the recession. The degree to which these problems fuel protectionist pressures in the United States will determine the intensity of the search for import restrictions—and the countervailing need for a political rationale to avoid them.

To the extent that American business, agriculture, and labor come to depend on exports for their livelihood, a broader coalition will emerge that has a stake in open world trade. They, too, will then be heard in Congress.

Observations on Current U.S.-Japan Trade Issues

YOTARO KOBAYASHI

THE IMPORTANCE of the Japanese-American dialogue on trade does not necessarily lie in new ideas or thoughts. It is almost as important to call for reinforcing actions already recommended or under way. That is what I propose to do.

Trade between the United States and Japan amounted to more than $60 billion in 1981, almost double the $33 billion of 1977. Except for Canadian-American trade, which is greatly facilitated by geography, this represents the most extensive bilateral trading relationship in the world. This huge volume of peaceful exchange is clearly of mutual benefit, or else it would not take place. Yet some recent statements about our trade must suggest to the casual observer that we are engaged in large-scale economic warfare.

An ominous tone in U.S.-Japan trade relations

What is a sensible American or Japanese citizen to make of the proposition that the military be used to help open the door to the Japanese market? Or that some aspects of Japanese culture be modified so as to accommodate American products or services? Some recent corporate advertisements directed at Japan's alleged unfairness remind one of the cheap military propaganda of prewar Japan, hardly up to the creative, sophisticated standards in the art of communication established by the American advertising industry.

At least as perceived by many Japanese, the American side of the recent trade dialogue has been dominated by exaggeration and extremism. Fortunately, as I see it, there has been no response in kind in Japan. I am uncertain as to whether this means that Americans are more concerned and Japanese less so about our current trade relationship. Or is it a reflection of differing cultures, one given to expressing its concerns in a highly vocal manner, the other quiet but perhaps hiding a deep resentment? I do not have the answer, but I do believe that we have cause for worry about the ultimate consequences that could flow from the unduly adversarial nature of our bilateral trade discussions. All of us bear a responsibility, it seems to me, to try to put the debate on a more sober and objective and less potentially inflammatory basis.

The substance of the bilateral trade problem, as presented by the United States, has undergone a series of shifts in emphasis. At an earlier point, tariffs and import quotas had the front of the stage. Later the exchange rate and nontariff barriers other than quotas received priority attention. Most recently, the focus has moved to industrial policy, or targeting. Market access has by no means become a nonissue, however, and it is well to consider it first.

Market Access

The most pervasive form of trade restriction, worldwide, is still the customs tariff. Taking into account recent reductions, Japan's average tariff level is 3.2 percent. This is lower than the averages of the United States and the European Community. As to import quotas, Japan restricts twenty-seven product categories by quantity, of which all but five are agricultural products, and most of these of minor trade importance. Elsewhere, France has twenty-seven quota-restricted items, West Germany eleven, and the United States six. In short, Japan's conventional import restrictions do not put it in a protectionist category by any comparative standard.

Nontariff Barriers

Many Japanese have been surprised and embarrassed to learn about nontariff barriers related to customs clearance procedures and to health, safety, and other standards or regulations. Most of these clearly should never have been allowed to develop or exist. It is a fact, however, that the government has taken a series of steps to eliminate the procedures or regulations that are not fully justified by considerations such as public health or consumer safety.

Japan's traditional multilayer distribution system is often cited as a nontariff barrier. I find it difficult to accept this view. The Japanese distribution system has evolved in conditions peculiar to Japan. It was not designed to exclude foreign goods or foreign firms. It is probably no more complicated than some distribution systems in Europe. A great many foreign as well as Japanese firms have been able to penetrate or to skirt the system effectively.

Another complaint is about "buy-Japanese" attitudes and practices. An example sometimes offered is the fact that few or no American automobiles are used by Japanese government officials.

This is not a particularly impressive example, since most other governments also seem to favor their local auto producers. More to the point is to observe the popularity in Japan of Levi jeans, Nike sneakers, McDonald's hamburgers, Mr. Donut's doughnuts, and Baskin-Robbins ice cream, or to visit an ultramodern integrated circuit factory in Kyushu where many of the tools and gauging instruments prove to be American made. Or, I can add, drawing from personal experience, Xerox products in reprographics have the largest share of the local and central government market in Japan, including the National Telephone and Telegraph Corporation.

Trade Study Group report

Unfortunately, much of what is said about the closed or open nature of the Japanese market, including my previous comments, is particular and anecdotal. A more comprehensive view of the matter is required and an excellent example is to be found in the report of the joint United States-Japan Trade Study Group, a body of representatives from government agencies and business organizations from both countries. The group's findings appear in a book compiled by the consulting firm McKinsey and Company under the title *Japan: Obstacles and Opportunities*. Among the salient points are the following:

1. The evidence suggests that American exporters and investors are being needlessly discouraged by misleading assumptions about Japanese business prowess and market entry problems.

2. Politicians and the press emphasize the U.S. merchandise trade deficit with Japan ($20 billion in 1982) while ignoring other measures such as the $20 billion of goods and services sold by U.S. companies operating in Japan (compared with $5 billion of sales in the United States by Japanese firms operating there), or the $21 billion of petroleum sold to Japan by U.S. oil companies, or the $2 billion to $3 billion in the 1980 U.S. services trade surplus with Japan.

3. Japan's imports of U.S. goods in 1981, at $22 billion, came to 1.9 percent of Japan's GNP, while Japan's exports to the United States, at $40 billion, represented 1.3 percent of the American GNP.

4. Although import barriers in the form of tariff and nontariff measures still exist, they are coming down gradually and steadily and are not insurmountable; they are not much worse than in other countries, including the United States; and they are much

less important than the lack of a greater U.S. effort at market penetration.

In the course of its work, the Trade Study Group examined the extent of American penetration of 126 manufacturing sectors and 195 wholesale, retail, and service industry sectors in Japan. Only 7 percent of the manufacturing sectors did not have a strong American representation in the form of wholly owned or joint venture firms. In 33 sectors, U.S. firms were among the top five leaders in market share.

Factors for success in the Japanese market, the Trade Study Group observed, include patience, imagination, and a willingness to tailor products to local needs and tastes. On the other hand, notable obstacles to success have been the failure to recognize and accommodate to the size and complexity of the Japanese market and to traditional Japanese business customs and practices. Many local managers of foreign firms in Japan attribute their most serious difficulties to misunderstandings in their head offices. (This headquarters syndrome is not a U.S. specialty; Japanese subsidiaries abroad commonly register very similar complaints about the lack of understanding and support from their home offices.)

The Trade Study Group's report reflects the results of a no-nonsense, public-private, binational inquiry. It is more than a listing of impressions or a compilation of grievances. It is in no way a whitewash of Japan. It is a balanced statement about a situation that is, I feel, often and widely misconstrued.

It is true that serious people, deeply concerned for Japanese-American relations, see the trade problem as one requiring further action by Japan on an urgent basis. Here is Ambassador Michael J. Mansfield, speaking recently in Tokyo:

> The most immediate and politically sensitive issue in U.S.-Japanese relations is unquestionably trade. . . .
>
> A situation now exists in which, in many different fields—manufactured goods, services, standard codes, investments—Japan enjoys easier access to the American market than America has to the Japanese market. In order to counter rising protectionist sentiment in the U.S. and among Japan's other major trading partners, Japan should, in its own interest, further open up her markets. For it is the widely shared perception that the Japanese market is not as open as it should be that is causing United States politicians—including previous champions of free trade—to call for new restrictions on imports from Japan. . . .
>
> I believe that these perceptions [that the Japanese market is not

accessible] will change further but only if trade liberalization continues in ways that lead to tangible changes in the ability of foreign companies to do business successfully in Japan.

Ambassador Mansfield's views are well respected in Japan and I certainly share this attitude. His is a voice of reason and integrity. All responsible Japanese will attend carefully to what he says. At the same time, I must record my personal opinion on this issue, summarized as follows.

There are still trade barriers in Japan that can be removed only at Japan's initiative. The agricultural and service trade sectors are ones in which Japan needs to move positively. But most of the tangible results referred to by Ambassador Mansfield must come from American initiatives, primarily in the private sector. These will require a strong commitment to the creativity and competitiveness required to take maximum advantage of a now much more broadly open door to the lucrative, if challenging, markets of Japan.

Industrial policy

A proposition that appears to be gathering great momentum is that Japan's so-called industrial policies, or industry targeting, represent strange and perhaps unfair efforts to gain advantages in international trade. It is not clear at this point whether the emphasis on industrial policy means that the arguments for greater market access have been depleted and a new basis for complaint is needed, or whether it reflects a genuine and new interest in learning from Japanese experience. Perhaps, as is most often the case, both motivations are present.

In one sense, industrial policy or targeting is no more than an effort to allocate and organize resources as rationally as possible. This is the fundamental problem of economics. It is what every private enterprise and every government seeks to do, by one means or another.

There is also, however, the tendency to look for something vaguely mysterious and conceivably duplicitous or illegal in industrial policy or targeting as practiced in Japan. I will offer an observation or two on this issue from a Japanese perspective.

On March 10, Mr. C. Fred Bergsten stated to the Subcommittee on Trade of the House Ways and Means Committee that "the success of Japan's industry targeting is . . . unclear." He went on to suggest four interesting subconclusions:

(a) There are numerous specific examples of Japanese efforts in this direction, and some evidence of its success in some industries.

(b) It is unclear how much impact there is at the overall trade or macroeconomic level, raising the issue of how widespread the effect of the practices may be.

(c) We simply do not know enough to come to firm conclusions. This is partly because of a classic "analyst's dilemma." Japan's repeated industrial successes can be explained *either* by its overall work ethic and undeniable competitiveness *or* by its industrial policies and government-business collaboration, and it is extremely difficult to sort out the relative importance of any single factor. Ambassador Brock may have been right when he suggested that the bottom line might not change even if Japan adopted every policy change urged upon it by the United States, but we really do not know.

(d) We, therefore, need much more study of the problem, especially concerning the relationship between the macro and micro elements of Japan's success. However, it may be that we will *never* come to a fully satisfactory answer to the question—because it may be inherently unanswerable.

Now when you find your competitor consistently outdoing you in the marketplace, despite your devoted efforts, the natural temptation may be to suspect unfair practice on his part. It is comforting, after all, to believe that you are losing not because of your own deficiencies but because the game itself has been rigged against you. This is an all too human reaction but not necessarily a productive one.

A case in my own experience is a new copier from a leading Japanese manufacturer that was beginning to sell extremely well in the United States. Volume was rising fast, prices were very attractive, and quality and performance were excellent. Xerox had reason for concern. Our initial reaction, in Japan as well as at U.S. headquarters, was to say that it was *unthinkable* that a product of that quality could be produced at costs to justify those prices and that therefore there must be something deceptive about our competitor's trade practices. What we found after careful study was that they were actually manufacturing the copier at a cost that was unthinkable according to Xerox's then-prevailing standards and were marketing it fairly and profitably worldwide.

The point is that there is nothing wrong about being or seeming to be different. It is never easy to accept being outperformed by someone "different." It is easy to assume that there is an element of artificial manipulation involved and to forget that new ways of doing things more efficiently are constantly being found.

One can remark, moreover, that the U.S. government itself frequently has targeted industries and goals: examples include military aircraft (with an obvious civilian spinoff), computers, spacecraft, and, for a century, the entire agricultural sector. It will be sensible, as Bergsten has suggested, to allow for further study, with appropriate comparative analysis, before coming to hasty and premature conclusions about Japan being either distinctive or unfair.

During the immediate postwar period and through the 1950s, Japan's government had a definite industry development policy, which included strict controls over imports and foreign exchange transactions, subsidies, tax reliefs, preferential loans for specific industrial sectors, and extensive intervention by the Ministry of International Trade and Industry (MITI) into private sectors.

In the 1960s direct interventionism gradually lessened. The shift was to "visions" for key industries. These were formulated by MITI with active participation by representatives from industry, labor, academia, and the press. They are not concrete plans or blueprints but rather statements of what are deemed to be desirable orientations for future industrial activities.

That the "visions" have an impact on the activities of individual firms and industries is undeniable. This is not because of their binding character, which does not exist, or because of MITI's authority. Their influence follows from their forecasting features, which of course are of interest to corporate managers and planners, and from the conspicuously conformist character of much of Japanese business.

MITI should be given credit for helping to shape today's Japanese industries, but certainly not, as popularly conceived in the West, as an awesome emperor presiding over Japan's industrial world. The ministry's real contribution has been as a supplier of timely, comprehensive, professional information about industrial and technological trends in Japan and worldwide.

Finally, a word about government subsidies for high technology. When and only when the development of new technologies is judged to entail an exceptionally long period or exceptionally high costs will the government participate financially. The Japanese government's share of total R&D spending, public and private, is about 27 percent. In the United States, defense R&D excluded, the government's contribution is 35 percent.

Conclusion   In a report prepared for the president of the United States and the prime minister of Japan in 1981, the Japan–United States Economic Relations Group offered some important and farsighted comments of a general nature:

> Japan and the United States are the two largest industrial democratic countries. They account for one-third of the world's annual production of goods and services and almost a fifth of its trade. . . . The continuing close economic, political, and security relationship of these two large countries is not only essential to their own national interests, but also to world peace and prosperity.

It continues,

> At the present time there is no highly politically visible on-going sectoral trade problem between them. Japan and the United States, however, cannot afford to be complacent about their relationship. Problems remain such as . . . a tendency for bilateral trade disputes to become highly politicized. The bilateral trade imbalance is currently at record levels and may well continue to widen in coming months, probably stimulating acrimonious debate on the openness of the Japanese market and the adequacy of U.S. export efforts. . . . Japan and the United States also face difficult, long-term challenges in strengthening their policies in support of liberalized trade and capital movements, in finding better means of anticipating and resolving bilateral economic disputes . . . and in improving their collaboration in a variety of ways to protect the international economic system and promote world peace.

The report then made a number of more specific points, including these:

—Japan's bilateral trade surplus is structural in nature; even the removal of all Japanese trade barriers would not eliminate the surplus. Countries should not be concerned about bilateral surpluses and deficits in trade or current accounts so long as their overall international payments are in long-term equilibrium, and countries need not even have a worldwide balance on current account to be in long-term equilibrium.

—Both countries, their consumers, and their agricultural communities will benefit from more liberalized trade and structural reform of the Japanese agricultural sector.

—The two governments should collaborate to generate a better data base on services and develop more sophisticated private-sector analyses of evolving service trade issues.

—Japan should continue to liberalize capital markets and encourage the internationalization of the yen. In the United States, state unitary taxation systems that discourage foreign investment and operate inequitably should be eliminated.

—As a comprehensive partnership, the Japan–U.S. relationship involves not only bilateral and reciprocal obligations but also shared responsibilities for the management of the international economic and political order. Each country needs to be cognizant of the interests and sensitivities of the other. Each needs to take these factors into consideration in its own policymaking process even when the issues are not directly bilateral in nature. Both Japan and the United States should seek to maximize Western European participation in international cooperation.

—To ensure an effective follow-up on the recommendations made, both governments should retain and utilize interagency mechanisms on a regular basis. There is a need for a continuing and constructive dialogue on difficult issues and there is a need for both governments and their private sectors to continue to monitor the relationship from a longer-term perspective, reviewing trade barriers and issues, assessing general trends, and seeking to identify future problems for more intensive work.

What else needs to be said to remind ourselves of the importance of our trade relations and of the things that have to be done to preserve them? Nothing, in my view, even today, a full year and a half since the report was published.

But, perhaps, as I said earlier, underlining and reiterating some of the key recommendations worked out through collaboration of experienced and responsible men from both sides such as the Japan-United States Economic Relations Group will not be without merit. And here I would like to set out in summary form a catalogue of commandments to be kept in mind.

—Both countries should remember that our partnership involves shared responsibilities for the world economic and political order.

—We should continue a constructive dialogue at various levels involving both the public and the private sectors.

—We should review trade barriers and issues regularly, hopefully with a mutually agreed-upon methodology of analysis and on the basis of mutually acceptable data bases.

—We should monitor the relationship from a long-term perspective, seeking to identify future issues and to prepare effective strategies for them on the basis of a mutually developed "vision" of our ideal trade relations.

—U.S. businesses should continue to strengthen their effort for higher productivity at home and greater competitiveness abroad.

—Our trade relationship is vital not only to the immediate interests of our two nations, but also to the future prosperity and peace of the world—East and West, North and South. It deserves and requires responsible and continuing attention.

General Discussion

WILLIAM CLINE of the Institute for International Economics commented that it is useful to look more closely at the degree of openness of the U.S. and Japanese economies. If one considers large sectors such as automobiles, steel—and in the past, television sets, textiles, and apparel—about one-third of the U.S. manufactured-goods market is covered by overt nontariff barriers. The corresponding figure for Japan would be less than 10 percent.

He added that this leads to the question of hidden barriers, and there we have to look at indirect evidence. One indicator is that the United States exports more to Japan than it does to Germany. It exports more manufactures to Japan than it does to Germany. It exports more electronic manufactures to Japan than it does to Germany. Then too, the ratio of Japan's imports to its GNP is higher than the United States' ratio, although that is about what one would expect based on the size of the Japanese economy. The composition of those imports is low in manufactures, but that is primarily because Japan has few indigenous raw materials, and must export manufactures to pay for raw materials imports.

We need to be wary also about resting a case on bilateral trade balances. If we use bilateral accounts as a criterion, the Europeans could say that the United States has high trade barriers against them because we have a large trade surplus with the European Community countries.

One may question as well reciprocity as a central strategy for our trade policy, Cline continued. Reciprocity, it can be argued, holds the seeds of protectionism within it, especially if administered by the wrong team at the top. If it were to be effectively implemented, it would require protection against an individual supplier on a non-most-favored-nation basis. This would be a blatant violation of Article I of GATT. It would risk retaliation, possibly on an escalating basis.

Senator Danforth replied that he agreed that there is two-way trade between the United States and Japan, but not necessarily a fair exchange. First of all, the United States has a substantial trade deficit with Japan, in the neighborhood of $20 billion in 1982. That represents a lot of American jobs. We tend to export raw materials and foodstuffs to Japan and get back automobiles. Value-added products come to us, while, generally speaking, we send raw materials the other way. This means jobs lost to American workers.

The senator went on to disavow any protectionist views. He said that the United States can compete not just in raw materials, but in manufactured goods as well—if given a fair chance to do so. He considered that U.S. trade strategy should be to obtain a fair opportunity to ship what we can make best into the Japanese market and to allow Japan to ship to us what it can produce most efficiently.

As for reciprocity legislation, Senator Danforth said, the theory is simply to catalogue barriers, not only in Japan but elsewhere in the world. As Kobayashi had said, we need to have a better understanding of facts. What are the facts? U.S. trade policy ought not to operate on the basis of anecdote. It surely ought not to operate on the basis of guesses. We have to try to quantify barriers to U.S. exports that do exist, and to try to get rid of them.

If we can get rid of them through negotiation within the GATT context, let us do so, but let us get rid of them, not just talk about the problem forever. Section 301 of the Trade Act of 1974 provides means of offsetting foreign barriers to our exports. It is in the law for a purpose and should be used.

Specifically in respect to U.S.-Japanese relations: Now, as in the past, we feel that we've been injured by Japan's import restrictions. We have anecdotes that tend to show injury. Therefore we send our politicians to Japan to complain. And it is not only one politician but a host of American politicians to be found in Japan complaining. It is demeaning to the United States and it is demeaning to Japan to plead and beg and complain about alleged barriers to international trade in this fashion. The object and the whole purpose of the reciprocity bill is to put our complaints on a nonrhetorical, systematic basis, and to work in a systematic way to remove them. None of this need mean a trade war, the senator concluded. The objective is not to raise barriers in the United States but to remove barriers elsewhere.

Lawrence Fox of the National Association of Manufacturers suggested that the reciprocity legislation might be improved if the U.S. government could be instructed to list its own barriers to American exports. This could take the form of reports from the Commerce Department and the U.S. trade representative as to the effect on export sales of the Export Administration Act and various other policies of our own government. To do that would help to provide balance in an assessment of the effects of foreign restrictions.

Kobayashi commented that it would be useful both to list domestic barriers to exports and, on a more positive basis, to compare the efforts on both sides to increase exports. Would it be possible, for example, to ask whether efforts on the part of the U.S. industries and companies to penetrate the Japanese market have been as sustained and imaginative as the efforts of their Japanese counterparts in the American market? In any case, it appears to be true that some government policies do discourage American exports. Ed Spencer of the Honeywell Corporation recently made a remarkable speech in which he listed twelve ways to increase the international competitiveness of U.S. industries, and among those were a number of things the U.S. government could do to improve the export climate for U.S. industries.

Fred Bergsten turned to the question of industrial policy and so-called industry targeting, which he characterized as a trade policy issue of growing concern in this country vis-à-vis Japan. While there is not enough present information to make a judgment about the aggregate impact of these Japanese efforts on trade, industrial policy is becoming a politically urgent issue. He felt that we should enunciate a principle that advanced industrial countries should not use infant industry protection, and that if subsidies clearly were being used, countervailing duties or other action should be taken against them. But he acknowledged that it is difficult for an outsider to get a firm grip on what is or is not the effect of Japanese industrial policy, and asked Kobayashi for his views on the matter.

Kobayashi gave a twofold answer: first, determining the actual effectiveness of industrial policy could best be attempted on a joint basis. This would be more persuasive, particularly if the study could establish a common data base.

His second point represented the point of view of a private businessman operating in a high-tech sector. The feeling in Japanese industry, as had been said earlier, is that MITI does provide a useful service in developing its so-called visions of what might happen in the more important technological sectors in the future, not only in Japan but worldwide. These visions, it should be noted, are compiled not solely by MITI, but with participation from other elements of the public sector and from the private sector as well.

The visions are not legally binding. MITI does not use them to determine the choices to be made by industries. But there is a rather remarkable tendency to conform on the part of many Japanese industries, something strikingly different from the situation in the United States. There are many exceptions, of course. Morita of Sony would surely disagree, as would Kobayashi of Nippon Electric. Still, among the hundreds and thousands of businesses in Japan, a prevailing conformist attitude means that the visions are taken by corporate planners as an important indication of what might happen in the future.

Former Secretary of the Treasury Henry Fowler referred to a study that addresses the issue of a widening gap between governmental support for specific industries in other countries and the absence of such policies in the United States. He asked Kobayashi for an opinion about the following recommendation in this study: "The United States Government should establish a sectoral research and information gathering capability to assess and evaluate industrial developments in the United States, the industrial policies of other countries, and their potential effect on U.S. industries, trade and employment."

Kobayashi replied that he would not wish to recommend anything to the U.S. government in the realm of industrial policy. He did recall the comments about industrial policy made by a Harvard Business School professor during a visit to Tokyo. The gist was that some of the criticisms in the United States about so-called industrial targeting in Japan make very little sense, since in any business the objective must be to apply resources according to some scheme of priorities, because some sectors are more productive than others. That is what the Harvard Business School teaches. That is the way to be competitive. That is the way to be effective. That is the way to survive.

Former U.S. Ambassador to Japan Robert Ingersoll observed that most industrialists in America believe that the exchange rate disparity between the yen and the dollar, rather than trade barriers, has been the greatest cause of the bilateral trade imbalance. Nevertheless, the impression persists among American businessmen that the Japanese market is not as open as the American market. Senator Danforth apparently had had that kind of comment from his constituents. Furthermore, the fact that Japan seems to be closed to other industrial countries' exports as well as to those from the United States might give credence to the belief that Japan is not quite as open a market as is sometimes asserted. Finally, a succession of market-opening packages coming after the government had persistently said that the market was entirely open does suggest that there had been a problem, just as foreign businessmen have said.

Ambassador Ingersoll continued by saying that there are structural changes taking place in American smokestack industries, regardless of imports, that are going to reduce employment, even if those industries reach the same levels of output in the future as in the past. He asked how these displaced workers were going to be redeployed to other industries. Or how is it to be explained to these workers that there may be a continuing unemployment problem in this industry, and that they probably are not going to be reemployed in their old jobs?

Kobayashi said that his answer to Ambassador Ingersoll would naturally be yes, that barriers have existed and perhaps do still exist. But he noted that the generalization should not be carried too far. He recalled a recent exchange with Mr. Ricci, the owner of Nina Ricci. To the direct question, "Mr. Ricci, do you have problems in Japan, do you find it very difficult to do business there?" the answer was "Yes, ten or fifteen years ago. But we have developed a very good relationship and today we have no problems, none."

It may well be, of course, that perfume is different from other manufactured goods, but the message from this incident is that difficulties can be overstated. Japan probably has not made a complete inventory of all the import problems that exist. But the doors are open wider. And actions have been taken by many American companies. It does take time, however, and patience is also necessary.

Senator Danforth agreed that the problem in the U.S. auto industry, for example, has causes other than imports. We have had a recession. The industry is moving to different methods of producing automobiles, and these have had effects on auto workers. But because of the recession and the other problems that that industry is experiencing, every additional straw put on the back of this particular camel seems all the more unbearable. The reason why there is so much concentration on the problem of imports is simply that people are out of work. If the economy were booming, imports would be less of a problem. And it is generally recognized in this country that we are never going to return to our old ways of making things. The smokestack industries are never going to be again the heart of the economy to the extent that they were in earlier times.

The theory of any import relief strategy now, such as the

urging of restraint in Japanese exports of automobiles to our country, is not to shut out Japanese imports permanently. It is to provide sufficient breathing room so that the industry can do the retooling necessary to be able to take reasonable advantage of whatever the market may provide. It is not possible to go back to where we were ten years ago, but at least we can try to keep alive a modern version of an auto industry in this country.

It is true that we must move increasingly to other lines of activity, high tech and services in particular, the senator added. Not everyone is going to be equipped to be employed in high tech. For those jobs that are available we're going to have to train people. We must emphasize training. Increasing attention is being given and must be given in our colleges and universities to the kind of scientific and mathematical education that we are offering our young people. Trade adjustment assistance is another of the keys, not in the sense of a welfare program, but as a program to retrain those who have been displaced, particularly those displaced by imports. Then too we must give greater attention to the service industries and to job opportunities that can be available in services, both in export terms and here at home.

The senator offered a final comment with respect to U.S. policy. The Congress, he noted, has been attempting to pursue policies that encourage savings, business investment, research and development, and consortia of American businesses to export or to operate abroad. Laws have been enacted and legislation proposed along these lines but it is certainly true that U.S. industry and the American people should not be taken off the hook. Even with the best possible policies, if our business community has no interest in doing business abroad or investing, if the sole interest is in next quarter's profit and loss statement, if there is no sentiment of get-up-and-go—on which we have prided ourselves historically—then government policy, no matter how well conceived, is not going to be adequate to the task.

It is much too soon, however, to give up on American industry and American labor, he said. Although we do have to keep the heat on our private sector to make sure that it is prepared to take advantage of opportunities that are available to sell what we make abroad, we still must address the problem of barriers in Japan and in other countries.

It is, therefore, a both/and situation, rather than an either/or situation. It is a mistake to put all of the blame on Japan or all of the blame on our government. It is also a mistake to say, "Well, really the problem is that we just lack the get-up-and-go spirit in

America and that there is no difficulty whatever with respect to import policies abroad."

Arthur Klauser of the Mitsui Company observed that it must be remembered that the United States was for over 150 years preoccupied with its domestic market. Senator Danforth and former Senator Adlai Stevenson were the original proponents of the Export Trading Company Act, which is a positive step toward educating American business to pay more attention to exports. But perhaps indifference to export markets is a larger real problem than the pockets of unemployment and the political problems that they cause. If we can continue to support export-oriented legislation and if the Congress can continue to provide policy incentives for business, then perhaps Americans for the first time in 150 years will take notice that there is a large market beyond our shores. Given the support of the government and the state governments and the business community, our export industries can begin to recover the trade position that we lost during the seventies.

Klauser recalled a Japanese saying to the effect that the frog in the middle of the well never sees the vast ocean beyond. He thought that the Export Trading Company legislation and the policies that Senator Danforth has proposed can help to bring the Fenton, Missouri, and the Mokena, Illinois, widgetmakers out of that well and into the vast area of international trade that is there for us to exploit.

An Official Perspective

Issues and Nonissues

WILLIAM A. NISKANEN

MY REMARKS TODAY are best described as reflecting the Council of Economic Advisers' perspective on U.S.-Japan economic relations. You will not be surprised to hear that there are several different perspectives within the administration on this issue. Our perspective, however, has been previously summarized in the *Economic Reports* and in congressional testimony with White House clearance.

Let me first explain our views on two dimensions of U.S.-Japan economic relations that are widely perceived to be problems: one is the substantial U.S. trade deficit with Japan, and the second is the exchange value of the yen.

The bilateral trade deficit

First, in general, there is no reason to be worried about a bilateral trade deficit unless one of two conditions apply. One is that there are overriding national security considerations, and the second is that the other country has a nonconvertible currency. In the present world, both conditions happen to apply typically to the same set of countries, but neither applies to Japan.

The U.S. trade deficit with Japan has been nearly equal to our trade surplus with Western Europe for many years, so it is a bit awkward for us to make an issue of such bilateral balances. It should now be clear that Japan's general trade position is primarily explained by conditions specific to Japan. The Japanese high saving rate is likely to lead to current-account surpluses for some time, which are likely to increase as restrictions on their capital markets are relaxed. It then becomes easier for foreigners to borrow in their capital markets and for Japanese to invest in the U.S. and other capital markets.

Japan's large surplus of manufactured goods is clearly due to its dependence on foreign supplies of oil, other raw materials, and a substantial amount of agricultural products. One of the ironies of the past decade is that increasing oil prices have strengthened the manufacturing competitiveness of oil-dependent countries and weakened that of oil-independent countries. The worst thing that ever happened to British industry was North Sea oil; conversely, the recent weakening of oil prices has strengthened its manufacturing competitiveness.

I sometimes wish that national governments did not collect balance of payments statistics, because it is not clear that they improve either private or public economic decisions. I would strongly oppose the development of balance of payments accounts among the American states, for fear that all of the wrong implications would be drawn from those accounts.

The exchange value of the yen

The so-called yen problem is best described as a dollar phenomenon, maybe even a dollar problem. The primary development in the exchange markets in the last two years has been an appreciation of the dollar against all currencies. In fact, the dollar has appreciated relative to the yen somewhat less than it has against other major currencies such as the German mark and the French franc. The yen is now stronger, relative to these other currencies, than it was two years ago.

We keep hearing stories that the government of Japan is manipulating the exchange rate to weaken the yen. The available evidence, however, is that the government of Japan has intervened rather heavily to support the yen in the last year, without substantial effect. We estimate that the yen is now undervalued by about 10 percent on a purchasing-power parity basis, somewhat less of an undervaluation than that of other major currencies.*

We should also recognize that several U.S. proposals that Japan open its capital markets more and reduce some of its restraints on agricultural imports, actions that we believe would be beneficial to both countries, would further weaken the yen. In general, it is unwise to allow our economic relations with any country to be dominated by a focus on the exchange rate.

The reasons why the dollar has appreciated so strongly in the past several years are not all that clear, in the sense that it is difficult to get consistent empirical answers. The most plausible reason for the strong dollar, as has been forcefully expressed by my colleague Martin Feldstein, is the large existing and prospective deficits, which have contributed to high real interest rates. Part of the crowding-out effect of large deficits is a crowding out in the trade sector. The combination of the strong dollar and the fact that we had a current-account deficit in the recession last year

*Ed. Note: For a somewhat higher estimate of the undervaluation of the yen, see McKinnon's paper.

was most unusual, but I think it is very likely attributable to the large existing and prospective budget deficits.

Another reason for the strong dollar, however, is not something made in Washington. The dollar, for all of the economic problems in the United States, is regarded as a safe haven by many people around the world. Property rights are not secure in many nations. In Mexico and France this past year, the banks were nationalized, property rights jeopardized, and exchange controls put on— actions associated with flights of capital to secure currencies like the dollar. I believe a significant cause of the strength of the dollar in the past year or so was the deterioration of property rights abroad.

Let me now turn to what I believe are real problems, as distinct from conditions like the trade deficit and the exchange value of the yen. We have a variety of real problems with Japan, but they are problems that can be resolved by a recognition of what our *mutual* interests are, rather than by unilateral action on our part.

Relaxing trade restraints The evidence is becoming increasingly clear that Japanese tariff and nontariff barriers on imports of manufactured goods have been brought down steadily and broadly over the past ten years. They are on the way to becoming among the lowest in the Western world.

Very severe restraints exist, however, on the importation of some agricultural products and on services. Over time we hope to convince the Japanese that it is in our mutual interest to relax those restraints.

A large part of the benefits from relaxing those restraints, however, will accrue to nations other than the United States. We have pressed the Japanese to increase their quotas on beef imports, for example. It is likely that a high proportion of any increased imports of beef by the Japanese would come from Australia, not from the United States.

But that general posture is consistent with our interests and those of Japan's other trading partners. We hope to convince Japan, recognizing the internal politics affecting agriculture and services, that it will be in its interest as well.

At the same time, such actions would weaken the yen and therefore worsen the competitive position of American manufacturing. In other words, relaxing trade restraints would lead to an increased specialization in areas of comparative advantage. Relaxing restraints on the importation of agricultural products and services would lead to a further sorting out on comparative-advantage lines among other sectors of trade.

Opening capital markets

Japan has progressively opened its capital markets over the years, but, for such a large nation, it still has a relatively closed capital market. The United States is in a position to make a case to the Japanese that it is in both our interest and their interest to relax the restraints on foreign borrowing in Japan and on Japanese investing in other countries.

Such action would contribute to equalizing real interest rates among countries, corrected for risk conditions. It would likely lead to a reduction of real interest rates in the United States, perhaps some increase in real interest rates in Japan, greater opportunity for Japanese savers to invest at higher returns, and greater opportunity for Americans and others to borrow in lower interest rate markets.

Again, this is an area in which our case to the Japanese is based on a mutual interest in pursuing change. It is also the type of action that, at least in the short run, would probably weaken the yen and therefore would not initially improve the competitiveness of American manufacturers.

Industrial policy

The United States also needs to sort out the effect of Japan's industrial policy on trade. Are the trade effects significant? Is Japan's industrial policy a basis for concern?

A line of reasoning has developed in the past half-dozen years that I believe is dangerous and that we should be careful to avoid. In effect, the argument goes that it is not in our interest to trade with countries that do not have economic policies or practices similar or nearly identical to ours.

A strict application of that standard would restrict trade between New York and California. It is dangerous to suggest that it is not in our interest to trade with countries that do not have similar economic policies, or economic history, or institutions, or even language. Differences among countries are in some sense trade barriers; they are also a basis for comparative advantage. We should be very careful not to let our lack of understanding about the consequences of Japanese industrial policy lead us into a stricter form of a reciprocity standard under which we restrict trade with countries that do not have regulations or antitrust policies or other economic policies like our own. I see little reason to export U.S. antitrust laws or regulations, and I am not sure that I would want to import those of any other country.

There are problems here. It is not clear what is an appropriate policy with respect to subsidies by foreign governments of their products. In general, subsidies by countries other than the most efficient producer may affect market share, but do not much affect market price. So there is little reason to be concerned in general about subsidies by countries that are in effect trying to buy market share in a world in which those subsidies don't have any direct effect on market price.

I also think that we should be prepared to live with subsidies that are in some sense a part of the permanent policy of another government, except in those conditions in which strong national security considerations dominate. By and large, if other governments over a sustained period of time choose to subsidize some particular good or service in international trade, a share of the benefits of such a subsidy will accrue to us.

A more difficult problem exists with respect to subsidies that are periodically put on and taken off and are in some sense unpredictable. It is not at all clear that American industries are more or less efficient if their property rights are protected from foreign subsidies. I have heard good cases made on both sides of that issue as to the effects on the efficiency of industry and of the economy as a whole. That issue simply needs further clarification.

An additional problem is that a subsidy is increasingly difficult to identify. This is particularly true in trade with countries in which there is a heavy state involvement in industry and with companies that are state-owned or state-controlled. This issue must be clarified in our own mind and through discussions on ground rules with our major trading partners.

Common defense concerns

Finally, there are very real problems in coordinating contributions to the common defense. The interests of our two countries in this area are nearly identical. There is no reason to question the commitment of either country to these shared goals.

One aspect of this problem involves the question of controls on the export of defense technology. West Germany and Japan are the two leading sources of technology imports by the Soviet Union. These two countries are our major allies in many areas, including defense. They are the two largest industrial democracies after the United States.

Japan and Germany are no less concerned than is the United States about the common defense, nor do they have less reason to be concerned about the security effects of trade in high-technology products with the Soviets. Nonetheless we have differences not only about exporting strategic goods and technology, but also about the respective size of budget contributions to the common defense. In any voluntary alliance such as NATO or the U.S.-Japan Security Treaty, or even a would-be cartel such as OPEC, there is an incentive for the smaller countries to count on the leading member to carry a disproportionate share of the load. That problem has been evident in the history of OPEC over the years, as it has been in the history of NATO. It is yet to be resolved.

American businessmen are concerned by the application of strategic controls on the export of their products or technology to the USSR or China or elsewhere when they see similar or identical technology being sold to those countries by competitors in allied countries. That is why an agreement on rules and a commitment to enforce them is necessary.

In conclusion, Japan is a valued friend, a valued ally, a valued trade partner, and a very strong competitor. The United States should avoid focusing on false issues that divide us—issues that have been in most cases created by misunderstanding, perhaps in some cases by special interests. It should also avoid dealing with them through unilateral approaches in which we try to elicit a response by the government of Japan to interests that apply to the United States alone. Instead our emphasis should be on issues that can be resolved in our mutual interest. Most of what I have described as the real problems in U.S. economic and trade relationships with Japan are of this nature. They can be resolved in our mutual interest if both countries recognize that interest and are conscientious in pursuing it.

General Discussion

HENRY OWEN said that a number of actions Niskanen suggested, notably liberalizing the Japanese capital market, would have the short-term effect of weakening the yen. Weakening the yen would strengthen Japan's competitive position in the United States and in third markets, which would increase protectionist pressures. In that connection he asked two questions. Would concern over this result be a reason to moderate at least the timing of Japan's measures to open its capital market? And, if not, what about the remedy suggested by McKinnon for obtaining a more realistic exchange rate, namely that the Federal Reserve Board should increase the U.S. money supply while Japan and Germany did not increase, or possibly restricted, their money supply?

Niskanen said he did not believe that an increase in the U.S. money supply would depreciate the real dollar exchange rate for any sustained period of time. It might have an immediate effect in that direction, but it is not clear that the real exchange rate is a function of monetary policy over periods of more than a year or so. He would be most reluctant to see either a substantial increase in U.S. money growth, which has already been at a very high rate since July 1982, or what would be the equivalent—a massive unsterilized intervention in the foreign exchange markets.

As to the liberalization of capital markets in Japan, Niskanen cautioned against trying to be too clever about timing. The process is one of convincing Japan that it is in its interest to take such action. That does not happen all at once and it cannot be carried out all that quickly. Furthermore, a case can be made that opening the Japanese capital market would strengthen the yen in the long run, because the yen would then be more likely to be used as an international currency. In part, what countries with strong currencies export is safe havens.

Robert Herzstein of Arnold and Porter agreed with Niskanen that trade between countries should not require that they have the same economic institutions. On the other hand, businessmen competing with each other for the same markets should expect to be subject to the same rules and to have the same opportunities and incentives open to them. Otherwise, the international system would be seen as unfair and would lose its legitimacy.

Niskanen said we have every reason to insist on a national treatment standard—for example, that American firms be treated like Japanese firms in the Japanese market. Conversely, Japanese firms have the right to insist on national treatment in the United States. That principle is wholly consistent with GATT. It is different, however, from the concept of reciprocity, which would require moves toward similar institutions in the two countries.

Strategic controls applied under Coordinating Committee (COCOM) procedures are a somewhat different matter. The problem applies to selling in other markets, most importantly the Soviet Union. We want to assure that business firms in the OECD countries are subject to the same rules in competing for such sales, although it is difficult to enforce those rules.

Herzstein asked why the underlying principle in the COCOM example should not apply to differences in the opportunities businessmen encounter in each other's markets. For example, American businessmen argue they are under a handicap because of differences between the Japanese and the American systems, such as the distribution systems, antitrust laws, and tax structures. We could posit perhaps an unrealistic example drawn from the automobile industry. Japanese automobile manufacturers were able to establish nationwide distribution in the United States within a relatively few years, even though the country is vast and outlets were needed in thousands of cities. One reason this was possible is that under U.S. antitrust laws existing dealerships of the American automobile companies could not be restrained from dealing in competing automobiles. The Japanese, therefore, were able to ride on the existing distribution system, rather than having to establish their own. Without arguing the point, suppose that under the distribution system in Japan private Japanese automobile companies could enforce restraints and impede foreign competitive opportunities. Would that not be a case for arguing that government policies toward the use of private restraints to impede foreign competition should be the same in both economies?

Niskanen thought not. Compare the treatment of U.S. and Japanese firms in the Japanese market and across the two markets. The United States should insist that Americans have as much freedom of entry in Japan as a Japanese firm would have in Japan. That may be less or more freedom than either has in the American market. There are some awkward rules in the United States, for example, that actually work in favor of Japan. It is easier for a Japanese bank to establish in California than it is for a New York bank to do so—a reverse national treatment standard.

But the fact that our distribution system, laws, antitrust policies, and regulations are different from those in another country is not a basis for trade restraint. It cannot be, because those differences will always exist, Niskanen maintained. Emphasis should, therefore, be on the strict application of a national treatment standard. In trade history, that was what the word "reciprocity" was originally used to describe. It applied to an extension to Germany of the national treatment standards in the British-French treaty of the 1860s.

Consequently, the fact that the U.S. distribution system is either more or less open than Japan's distribution system is not relevant. A basis for concern exists only if the Japanese distribution system is more closed to American firms than to Japanese firms.

Herzstein said that he was not necessarily suggesting that these kinds of differences should be used as a basis for imposing trade restraints. They should serve, however, as a challenge to lead policymakers toward a harmonization of the rules. Businessmen in different countries are competing for the same customers; it is understandable they should ask to compete on the same basis.

Niskanen would consider differences in industrial practices and government policies a basis for a scholar's attention in the sense that they provide insights about relative effectiveness. There is a great deal for the United States to learn from Japan about industrial practices and, in some cases, government policies. That doesn't by itself mean that policies should be harmonized. Any given policy or practice could be best for one country and not for others.

He saw no strong reason to harmonize such policies and in general was critical, for example, of attempts, usually through OECD, to coordinate macro policies among countries in one direction or the other. He believed such attempts are politically unrealistic and likely to be economically dangerous.

MacLaury asked whether the additional demand for the dollar arising from its safe-haven function should not cause the Federal Reserve to provide for holding these dollar assets without causing interest rates to rise or the exchange rate to strengthen on that account. He also asked why, in discussing an agreed approach to the common defense, Niskanen had not given more emphasis to the very different proportions of GNP expended on national defense in Japan and the United States and any implications this might have for relative economic performance.

Niskanen responded that if the actual inflation rate is equal to the target inflation rate, and demand for dollars increases, the United States probably should increase the supply of dollars. Otherwise, the inflation rate will come in lower than the target rate.

Failing to sterilize this external demand for dollars, however, would not necessarily be wrong. For example, there has been a large increase in the demand for dollars in the past year, in part coming from abroad. However, two years ago the United States had a very high inflation rate. The increase in the external demand for dollars brought inflation down more than domestic monetary policy by itself would have done, but that is not clearly a wrong outcome.

If the objective is to get down to a 5 percent inflation rate and there is an increased external demand for dollars, the prior money path might reduce the inflation rate below the target. If you want to make sure of at least 5 percent inflation, then increase the money supply. But someone else will have to defend that point of view.

There are other consequences, of course, Niskanen added. A strengthening of the dollar hurts our manufacturing sector and results in higher unemployment. Increased external demand for dollars, not offset by monetary policy, therefore entails costs.

Agreement on rules relating to the common defense is based on a number of factors, including respective budgetary expenditures on military forces. The U.S. position of encouraging Japan to spend more for defense is a little awkward, because Japan is constrained by a constitution that was very largely of American origin.

*Capital Flows
and Financial Policies*

The Yen Rate and the Tokyo Capital Market

MICHIYA MATSUKAWA

ECONOMIC FRICTION between the United States and Japan arises for various reasons, but the American perception of the cheaper yen is certainly a major one. Therefore, it may be well to begin by introducing the factors that have been affecting the yen's exchange rate and by explaining how the Japanese see the foreign exchange rate issue.

There is a widely held belief in the United States that Japanese monetary authorities have been manipulating the exchange market in order to keep the value of the yen down, so as to make Japanese exports more competitive in international markets. This is a fundamental misconception of the real situation. To show why this is so I would like to illustrate how in fact the value of the yen was determined during 1982.

First I would like to point out three important facts regarding the movement of the yen in 1982.

1. The value of the yen was relatively stable in 1982 with respect to major European currencies, especially the German mark and the Swiss franc, but fluctuated wildly with respect to the U.S. dollar.

2. The value of the yen depreciated, but, contrary to the general belief that the cheaper currency would help to increase exports, Japan's exports did not rise but rather fell—in volume as well as value.

3. There was a large deficit of about $5 billion in the overall balance of payments for Japan. The deficits in both the capital account and the services account were not offset by the surplus in the trade account.

The yen-dollar rate

The rate of the yen vis-à-vis the U.S. dollar kept falling throughout the first ten months of 1982. The cheaper yen caused a good deal of frustration among Americans who were suffering from recession, a high rate of unemployment, and a large trade deficit with Japan. This does not mean, however, that the yen was too cheap but rather that the dollar became too expensive throughout 1982,

83

mainly due to Federal Reserve policies that kept American interest rates high.

At the beginning of 1982 the rate was 218.20 yen to 1 dollar. This was the peak for 1982. After declining continuously for ten months, it hit bottom early in November at 277.65 yen to the dollar, or a devaluation of more than 21 percent during this period.

But the rate of depreciation of the yen was much smaller against the German mark. The yen hit a peak at the beginning of 1982 at 98.00 yen to 1 mark and fell to a bottom late in October at 109.46 yen. The pattern of movement of the yen's value in relation to the mark was almost the same as that to the U.S. dollar, but the rate of depreciation was only around 10 percent, half the rate of depreciation against the dollar.

Against other major European currencies, the yen grew stronger toward the end of the year. It hit a peak against the Swiss franc in late November, having appreciated 11 percent from its low in March. It hit peaks at the end of the year vis-à-vis both the British pound and the French franc, after appreciating gradually. The rates of swing from the bottom to the top in 1982 were 18 percent for the pound and 13 percent for the French franc. Generally, the record of changes in the yen rate during the first ten months of 1982 shows that the dollar was the currency that registered the widest fluctuations and became exceptionally strong relative to the yen.

Because the U.S. dollar is the currency commonly used in the export contracts of Japan, the yen-dollar rate has paramount significance for Japan's international trade. The depreciation of a country's currency is generally believed to bring a relative advantage in international markets for the goods produced by that country. This presumes that the country with the weaker currency must be able to export a greater quantity of goods, if not a larger monetary amount. But this theory did not hold in the case of Japan in 1982. Even when the yen became weaker, exports still shrank.

Statistics compiled by the customs authorities show that: (1) the total amount of exports from Japan in 1982, $139 billion, was 8.7 percent below the previous year's level. On a quarterly basis, the rate of decline from the previous year's level continuously widened from 0.2 percent in the first quarter to 15.1 percent in the fourth quarter; and (2) this 8.7 percent decline in exports was attributable to a decrease in the export volume of 3.0 percent and a fall in the average unit price of 5.8 percent.

Although exports declined by $12 billion in 1982, the current-account surplus increased by $2 billion because of a $10 billion decrease in imports and a $4 billion decrease in the deficit in services. The increase in the current-account surplus would have been expected to push up the yen rate vis-à-vis the U.S. dollar, but instead the yen weakened. This happened because of the extremely large outflow of capital from Japan.

Japan's capital account

Total international capital transactions in Japan in 1982 showed a net outflow of $16.5 billion ($15 billion in long-term capital and $1.5 billion in short-term capital). This huge deficit in the capital account created an overall balance of payments deficit ($5 billion) and made the yen rate weaker. The magnitude of the capital outflow in 1982 was at a record high. Its effect on the exchange market was somewhat greater than anticipated. It may be useful, therefore, to comment on the flow of capital, especially long-term capital, into and out of Japan.

Until the mid-1960s, Japan was a capital-importing country. The current account in the balance of payments was always in deficit and there was not enough domestic capital to meet the growing demand for economic development. But as of 1965, as the current account broke out of its deficit position and as foreign exchange controls were gradually relaxed, Japan became a capital-exporting country.

As Japan's direct investments abroad have grown in order to expand and geographically diversify business activities and as loans to foreign borrowers have increased, the amount of net capital outflow has been over $1 billion in each year since 1970 (except 1975). In both 1978 and 1979 net capital outflow exceeded $12 billion.

Against this background, the government decided to liberalize foreign exchange controls, which had been maintained throughout the postwar period. At the beginning of 1981 all transactions related to foreign exchange were liberalized. Having awaited this liberalization, Japanese capital started flowing outward on a large scale from the middle of 1981, seeking better opportunities in foreign stocks and bonds in addition to direct investments and loans.

It is pertinent to observe that in 1982 the amount of outflow of long-term domestic capital varied little over the course of the year, remaining at about $7 billion in each quarter. On the other hand, the inflow of foreign long-term capital was rather small in the first three quarters, reaching only around $2 billion, and then

jumped in the fourth quarter to $6 billion as interest rate differ-
entials started narrowing.

The large capital outflows over the past several years have made
Japan one of the most important capital-exporting countries. The
total outstanding amount of Japan's claims in foreign countries
exceeded $200 billion at the end of 1981. This amount is still less
than 30 percent of total American claims, but it is nearing the
West German figure.

What is surprising is the rapidity of growth of capital transactions in securities and loans over the past ten years. The tempo
of this growth has been accelerating since the beginning of 1981.
In one year, 1981, the following outflows were recorded: (1)
investments in foreign securities grew from $21 billion to $31.5
billion; (2) long-term loans rose from $12 billion to $19 billion;
(3) short-term monetary assets in the private sector went from
$45 billion to $61 billion; and (4) direct investments increased
from less than $20 billion to almost $25 billion.

Outstanding liabilities, that is, foreign investment in, and loans
to, Japan, have also increased rapidly. The changes in 1981 were:
(1) foreign investments in Japanese securities grew from $45 billion
to $68 billion; and (2) short-term borrowings by Japanese grew
from $78 billion to $100 billion.

In short, various types of capital transactions affecting the yen
became extremely active during 1981. This trend was due primarily
to the liberalization of foreign exchange controls. It has continued,
if not intensified, through 1982.

*International
financing*

I would like next to touch on the role of the Tokyo capital market
in international financing. The liberalization of foreign exchange
controls has made the Tokyo capital market very important to
foreign borrowers. In 1980, just before liberalization, the Tokyo
market could provide yen-denominated bonds for foreign issuers
equivalent to about $1.1 billion, or about 2.6 percent of the total
foreign bonds floated in all international capital markets that year.
This amount does not include capital obtained by foreigners in
the form of syndicated yen loans amounting to $820 million.

In 1981, the first year after the liberalization, the total amount
of yen-denominated bonds rose to $2.5 billion, about 4.6 percent
of the total international bond market. When syndicated yen loans
are added, the amount financed in the Tokyo capital market
reached $4.6 billion. In 1982 yen-denominated bonds increased
further to $3.4 billion, 4.5 percent of the global total. With
syndicated yen loans, the total rose to $8.1 billion.

The access of foreign borrowers to the Tokyo capital market is now fully liberalized and is no longer subject to government control. As in other capital markets, the Japanese government seeks to protect the interests of investors by regulating the quality of bonds and by requiring full disclosure of information about issuers. In all other aspects, the bond market is virtually free of government control.

Nevertheless, one limitation on access to the Tokyo capital market still exists. It arises out of the rush to Tokyo by too many candidates seeking to issue yen bonds. In 1981 the amount of foreign yen bonds floated on the Tokyo market increased so fast that their share in the primary market in Japan reached 4.4 percent, which is much higher than the estimated 2.7 percent share of foreign bonds in the American market. However fast the Tokyo market is growing and however strongly its participants desire to make it one of the key markets in the world, the market itself cannot digest sudden surges in demand by foreign borrowers. Thus a certain amount of traffic control has been introduced to the market by a managing underwriters' group, which is seeking to place a ceiling on the number of flotations and the total amount involved.

In the past, the yen has not been an important reserve currency. For instance, in 1975 its share of the currencies held by world monetary authorities was only 0.5 percent. Since then, with the two oil crises, the economy of Japan has shown its resilience to external shocks by maintaining relatively stable growth. In this climate, the yen became stronger. When the dollar lost its predominance in the world monetary market in the late 1970s and the dollar standard was in question, the role of the yen as an international reserve currency increased and its share among the currencies held by the world monetary authorities rose to 4.1 percent by the end of 1981. It became the third most important reserve currency after the dollar and the deutsche mark.

The internationalization of the yen has been expedited primarily by a rapid buildup in yen holdings by nonresidents. There are various reasons for this. Under the floating-rate system, where wild swings in exchange rates could not be avoided, holders of petrodollars and other fund managers diversified their assets. Economic fundamentals in Japan have been brighter relative to those in almost any other country, and politically and socially Japan is known as being very stable and solid.

We cannot overlook some other important reasons lying behind this rapid buildup in yen holdings. There is a first-class money and capital market in Japan, both in quality and magnitude, which offers good opportunities in investment and financing. In 1980, for instance, the total value of outstanding bonds on the Japanese market was less than half that of the American market but more than twice that in Germany, and the total amount of bonds turned over in Japan was also the second largest in the world. Stocks listed on the Tokyo Stock Exchange have a total value of about half that of the New York stock exchanges and more than double that of the London exchange.

Yen claims held by nonresidents (including monetary authorities) are now estimated to total more than $100 billion up to the end of 1981, out of which about $30 billion is made up of claims in Euroyen. This amount must have also increased in 1982, but the actual figure is not yet available.

The role of the yen as a currency for storing value has greatly increased in recent years. Yet it still remains a minor currency for settling international transactions. Even with respect to exports from Japan, only 17 percent of all export contracts were denominated in yen in 1975 and 32 percent in 1981. In the case of imports into Japan, only 1 percent was denominated in yen in 1975 and close to 3 percent in 1981. No contract between third countries is believed to be denominated in yen. Thus the use of yen as a settlement currency in international trade is still negligible, and its future role in this respect will remain very small unless something extraordinary emerges in the international monetary system.

Exchange rate system In response to these underlying forces, especially the increase in capital transactions after the liberalization of foreign exchange controls, the exchange rate of the yen has been continuously and widely fluctuating. This has brought complaints among Japanese about the wisdom of maintaining the floating-rate system itself. For example, in the public hearing of the Diet on the budget bill in February 1983, Akio Morita, chairman of the Sony Corporation, spent most of his time explaining the undesirable effects of unstable exchange rates on business activities and then requested a review of the present foreign exchange system so as to introduce greater stability. A growing number of businessmen in Japan are joining in this criticism against the floating-rate system, which is generally blamed for the excessive volatility in the yen's exchange rate.

However, no one has an easy answer to the problem of bringing greater stability to exchange rates. Some suggest introducing a European Monetary System type of arrangement. Some suggest a target-zone system, and others, a wider band system. Whatever the feasibility of any one of these systems, a way to bring increased stability to the exchange market has definitely become a high priority.

In any event, we must face the reality of capital transactions playing a predominant role in determining exchange rates. I am rather skeptical that the world's leading democracies can effectively insulate the exchange market from the pressures of capital movements or from the influence of currency speculation. If they, in fact, cannot, it may be extremely difficult to reestablish an international monetary system in which exchange rates are relatively stable. Cooperation among the leading countries, in both macroeconomic policies and government exchange market intervention policies, may eventually be accepted as the only practical means available to curb the volatility in exchange markets.

Conclusions

Japan's international trade balance in 1981 showed a large surplus, and the bilateral balance between the United States and Japan was greatly in favor of Japan. Nevertheless, the yen rate was weak against the U.S. dollar throughout 1981. These developments have made Americans suspect that the Japanese authorities have been taking measures in the foreign exchange market to make the yen weaker. But as I have pointed out earlier, the decline in the value of the yen was caused by deficits in the overall balance of payments and a shortage of dollars in the foreign exchange market. These had their origin in the huge net outflow of capital from Japan.

Why was the net capital outflow from Japan so large in 1982? Large capital outflows have taken place since late in the 1970s. They accelerated during and after 1981 when foreign exchange restrictions in Japan were completely liberalized, including those relating to capital transactions. Liberalization of international investment at the beginning of 1981 was the trigger for additional capital outflows from Japan and the main cause of the cheap yen in 1982.

History shows that when a country becomes stronger economically its international trade balance turns to a surplus and it begins to export capital. This sequence also applies in the case of Japan. Since Japan's trade accounts, merchandise and services together, turned to a surplus in 1965, Japan has been continuously exporting capital. Some has been related to the export of merchandise in the form of suppliers' credit, and some has been in the form of economic assistance to developing countries. Direct investments abroad have also increased. The scale of these capital flows, however, was too small to have much effect on the exchange rate.

Suddenly in 1981 and thereafter, net capital outflow from Japan increased rapidly, mainly because of the increase in loans to foreign borrowers and Japanese investments in foreign equities and bonds. The main reasons for this sudden increase have been the strong demand for loans by foreign governments and other borrowers and the wide interest differentials between yen- and dollar-denominated securities. After waiting for liberalization, all these potentials for Japanese capital outflow materialized in a relatively short period. The tempo of the outflow was so rapid that it weakened the yen rate.

In conclusion, I would like to say that the volume of capital outflow from Japan will not be rising much in the years to come, and capital inflow into Japan will increase again as interest rate differentials narrow and as international anxiety over the world's political and financial situation lessens. This will help to eliminate undue pressure on the yen and return the exchange rate to an appropriate level.

External and Internal Balance in Japan's Financial Policies

ANTHONY M. SOLOMON

I AGREE with most of Matsukawa's comments on capital flows and external capital markets, but I also have some reservations.

First, Matsukawa points out correctly that the volume of Japanese exports declined in 1982 even though the yen was alleged to be cheap. But this should not be viewed as surprising. There are several reasons why there would have been a decline in Japanese export volume in 1982. There are lags in the adjustment of trade flows to currency changes. There was a world recession in 1982, and imports by developing countries and OPEC countries (heavily skewed to Japanese goods) were especially hard-hit. Furthermore, various industrial countries' "voluntary" import quotas on Japanese goods were biting. These reasons would be enough to explain why the volume of Japan's exports declined even with an undervalued yen.

Second, Matsukawa also pointed to the fact that the share of foreign borrowing in the Japanese bond market is larger than the comparable share of foreign borrowing in the U.S. bond market. I wonder if that's the most relevant comparison, since it ignores the Eurodollar bond market. A very large share of foreign dollar-denominated bond issues is placed in the Eurodollar bond market, which is beyond U.S. control. By contrast, the Euroyen bond market is very small and is kept under close control by the Japanese monetary authorities.

Are large Japanese current-account surpluses inevitable?

I would like to turn now to the broader topics considered at this conference. First, even though I accept the fact that Japan, on the whole, will run current-account surpluses, I do not believe it is inevitable that they will be very large or exist all the time. In five out of the past eleven years Japan has been in deficit. The cumulative current-account surplus over the past decade or so was fairly modest in size, about $25 billion. Therefore, although it is probable that Japan will run current-account surpluses in the future (like other industrial countries), they do not have to be disruptively large, given proper domestic policies.

91

I recognize that there is a view that Japan must show a large current-account surplus because it has a high domestic private savings rate *and* that savings rate is not responsive to government policies. I question that view because I believe that in the long run the savings rate is influenced importantly by government policies.

The United States does not have the right to criticize the Japanese life-style preference for high saving. It has the right, however, to criticize restrictions in the domestic financial markets in Japan or market conventions (often sanctioned by the Japanese authorities) that make it difficult and expensive for families to secure credit. As domestic financial deregulation continues in this area, as it should, ordinary Japanese citizens, especially young families, will find it much easier to acquire household durables. In the meantime, the result is to restrict consumption and artificially push up the savings rate. (Incidentally, the notion that Japanese citizens have all the gadgets they need is simply untrue. International comparisons still show Japan well behind most high-income European countries and far behind the United States in per capita ownership of various consumer goods.) Furthermore, the under-developed state of the home mortgage market and agricultural subsidies that raise the price of land make housing more costly and thus also discourage spending and encourage saving.

There is a growing body of opinion within Japan which recognizes that continued liberalization of financial transactions on the international side while retaining constraints and restrictions on domestic financial markets can produce an unbalanced economic outcome. I believe that Japanese domestic markets will inevitably be deregulated, but perhaps the process could be speeded up because it is causing problems on the international side.

It is also worth pointing out that Japan may not need a persistently large trade surplus in the future to cover a large deficit in international services transactions. Japan's services deficit will likely begin to shrink in the next few years. For one thing, Japan probably will reverse its position as a net payer of royalties for technology and other know-how and will increasingly become a receiver of royalties and fees. At present, royalties and fees account for some $5 billion out of a total deficit of $10 billion for services transactions in 1982. In addition, Japan's transport deficit may also narrow as Japanese firms take over more business. And Japan's net investment income from abroad *must* improve as it continues to run current-account surpluses and thus increases the volume of its investments abroad.

Still, the combination of a relatively competitive yen and a declining services deficit seems destined to produce sizable current-account surpluses for at least the next several years or so. The question arises: how will they be recycled—directly through Japanese private and public institutions or indirectly through intermediaries abroad? The concern that Japan's current accounts cannot be loaned and invested through Japanese financial institutions seems to me to be misplaced. The gross financial flows into and out of Japan are already very large, running close to $100 billion for 1983, by our calculation. So to get a net capital outflow of $20 billion to offset what might be this year's current-account surplus should not be difficult. Moreover, these gross financial flows are larger, on the whole, than for Germany and many other industrial countries. For example, Japan's total long-term capital exports have been twice as large as Germany's in the last two years. Japan has exported around $90 billion of long-term capital in the past five years.

The real problem is not the extensiveness of the financial links Japan has with the rest of the world but the existence of the serious domestic financial obstacles I pointed to earlier that are contributing to a larger current-account surplus than the world may need.

Let me turn next to the question of the yen. First, I am not persuaded that greater internationalization of the yen will automatically lead to a stronger yen over time. It depends on a lot of other factors and the outcome could go in either direction. Right now, when Japanese interest rates are low, it would probably mean greater foreign borrowing of yen, which would actually weaken the currency as the borrowed yen are converted to dollars or other currencies.

Second, it is probably unwise to single out Japan as a special problem in the exchange markets. Instability is part of a worldwide problem, and there are going to continue to be strong swings in current-account surpluses and deficits in response (after lags) to exchange rate strengths and weaknesses.

We may, however, continue to experience an increasing volume of noneconomically motivated capital flows, which could produce exchange rates that may represent equilibrium from the point of view of capital flows but not from a trade point of view. I am not sure what could be done about that except to limit the damage somewhat, if there is enough international cooperation.

Looking ahead, I would assume that the yen exchange rate will ultimately respond to Japan's persistent current-account surplus.

I would also assume that the dollar exchange rate will respond to persistent deficits in the U.S. current account, unless that factor is swamped by capital inflows, including those inspired by political developments—that is, money seeking a safe haven. Indeed, if safe-haven considerations become so dominating, and do so much damage to trade and economic output, it may become necessary to take somewhat less of a free market attitude toward capital movements.

To sum up, I want to emphasize again that no country can have external balance without internal balance. Japan cannot live indefinitely with increasing financial liberalization on the international side and a very restrictive situation in the domestic financial markets. In my opinion, that imbalance is disruptive and damaging to the Japanese economy, and it certainly does not help the world adjustment problem. There is more that Japan can do in this general area, and I would assume that we will see, over time, a correction of the exchange rate, which has been the subject of so much concern.

General Discussion

MAC LAURY NOTED that both Matsukawa and McKinnon had argued that the high value of the dollar relative to the yen and to other currencies over the past two years was largely a reflection of the tightness of U.S. monetary policy. He asked whether Solomon agreed with that analysis.

Solomon said he believes that interest rate differentials are a major determinant of exchange rate movements, although the correlation has not been strong in the short run and its importance varies from currency to currency. In his view, exchange rates should be factored into the consideration of domestic monetary policy. However, he found it difficult to imagine a world in which domestic monetary policies are based entirely on international factors and money supply targets are coordinated among the key countries, as McKinnon suggests. It is difficult enough to understand what the domestic money supply is, let alone control it. He was skeptical that monetary authorities would be capable of making accurate assessments to respond to shifts in the international demand for assets. That doesn't mean that we should not be very aware of the information that the exchange markets give us about monetary policy and factor it in. More of that should be done in considering U.S. monetary policy.

MacLaury, referring to Solomon's argument that liberalization of external capital flows was incompatible with continued management of domestic money and capital markets, asked Matsukawa what financial controls still existed in Japan. Or if the controls are not explicit, he asked, what restrictions or guidelines apply to the use of credit, such as the committee to which Matsukawa had referred that apparently must approve foreign capital issues floated in Tokyo?

Matsukawa said that this system, in which a group of underwriters regulates the total amount of bonds to be floated in certain months, is not unique to Japan. In Switzerland, the three leading banks serve a similar function. At present, the number of applications to float bonds in Japan is beyond the capacity of the primary bond market to digest. Some traffic control is necessary, among other reasons, in order to assign priority to the issues of the international development banks, notably the World Bank and the Asian Development Bank. Private corporations have to wait their turn in the queue.

Solomon said he was referring mostly to the domestic capital market in Japan—specifically to the restraints on the consumer loan industry and to the fact that the home mortgage market is underdeveloped. These constraints discourage spending and encourage saving, which in turn is a factor in creating the current-account surplus. Liberalization of the international capital market is proceeding at a satisfactory pace, but constraints on domestic credit could create problems for the international system.

Matsukawa replied that the interest rate structure is hierarchical and too rigid. National government bonds have to be rated better than local government bonds, which in turn are rated better than corporate bonds, and so on. Notes floated by the Japanese Industrial Bank have their own special place. Years ago differentials among those rates were wide; now they are very close to each other.

Even domestic borrowers find the system too rigid, but changes would cause profits or losses to various banking institutions, depending on their role. Financial "wise men" such as former governors of the Bank of Japan have been asked for suggestions about how to improve the situation. They are meeting on the problem but it will take time to change procedures and liberalize interest rates, since some will benefit and some will have to sacrifice. That foreign borrowers coming to Japan should find the system inconvenient is understandable, because most Japanese feel the same way, Matsukawa said. In the meanwhile, the secondary market is basically uncontrolled.

McKinnon agreed with Solomon's assessment of tensions in Japanese financial markets. With exchange controls removed and interest rates managed, achieving a correct balance between the current-account surplus and capital overflow in the economy requires queuing or rationing credit to foreign borrowers. At the present time, queuing has not prevented a large capital outflow from Tokyo, which has resulted in a weak yen.

Japanese authorities are loath to get rid of interest rate management this year because world interest rates are so high, particularly those in the New York capital market. The way out, McKinnon said, is a deal whereby the Federal Reserve expands money sufficiently in the United States to bring the dollar down against the yen, which would mean lower American short-term rates of interest. The Bank of Japan could stand fast, not expand, and largely eliminate restrictions on interest rates in Japan.

Lawrence Fox of the National Association of Manufacturers commented that the safe-haven demand for dollars could make the dollar intolerably strong in trade-related terms, thus increasing pressure for trade restrictions. If so, he asked Solomon, should not offsets be created to limit the strengthening of the dollar for this reason? Or is the risk of such safe-haven effects too small to warrant any major change in the international monetary system?

Solomon agreed that if political safe-haven flows should continue, which seems likely, some kind of action in the capital and monetary area might be required. However, the problem may in fact turn out to be quantitatively manageable through corrective action normal to the system.

Yoshitomi commented that he did not see a positive relationship between interest rate regulation in the primary market and excess savings in Japan. Regulations result in interest rates being lower than otherwise, which should cause people to save less. Indeed, interest rates are regulated in the primary market, but they are all uncontrolled in the secondary markets. International investors can use these secondary markets freely, both for short- and long-term investments. It is difficult therefore to see the connection between regulated interest rates in the primary market and external capital flows.

Solomon replied that the fact remains that interest rates in Japan tend to be impervious to the movements of rates in the international short-term capital and money markets, which causes a problem for the system. McKinnon and he are agreed on that point. This failure of rates in Japan to move toward the international level has to be the consequence of constraints imposed by Japanese monetary authorities and the guidance they provide the market. Furthermore, the high cost of consumer credit and the underdeveloped state of that industry in Japan discourage the purchase of durables by Japanese and tend to encourage saving.

Matsukawa sought to clarify the extent to which interest rates are rigid in Japan. Three different types of interest rates are in this category: the interest rate on deposits with the Postal Savings Office; the rediscount rate of the Bank of Japan; and the rate on national bonds. The rate on national bonds is reviewed each month; the other two rates can be changed at any time by the respective authorities.

Each of these three rates is bound to limit the movement of

related rates. For instance, the rate on deposits with the commercial banks is influenced by the rate on Postal Savings deposits; lending activities of the commercial banks are more or less linked with the rediscount rate; and rates in the long-term capital markets are influenced by the rates on national bonds.

On the other hand, as Yoshitomi has noted, all other interest rates, including those on the secondary bond markets, are completely free. Thus, the rigidity of interest rates applies only to certain categories and instruments. There are many exceptions. It is mistaken therefore to view interest rates as being rigidly determined by monetary authorities.

Thomas Atkinson of the General Motors Overseas Corporation asked Matsukawa whether Japan really wanted to internationalize the yen. A few years ago that did not seem to be the case. He also asked: (1) Was it proper for the United States to seek to influence Japan in removing controls on capital markets, or was this an area where, as Niskanen had argued earlier, each country had a right to maintain its own rules for its own markets as long as foreign participants received national treatment? and (2) Did Solomon believe, as his remarks implied, that internationalization of the yen would not increase its value?

Matsukawa replied that officials of the Ministry of Finance or the Bank of Japan do not want to see the internationalization of the yen take place too rapidly. They know that internationalization of the yen would weaken their ability to control monetary policy and the money aggregates. At the same time, they also recognize that the integration of the world economy is a continuing process, and, like it or not, the currency of Japan will have to be used freely in the international arena. Thus despite their inclinations to the contrary, the stance of monetary authorities is to accommodate the process of internationalization by not placing obstacles in the way. That is why they agreed to liberalize capital control in late 1980. All this means that the internationalization of the yen is a natural step in global development, in both an economic and monetary sense.

Solomon said he found much less resistance in Japan to the yen's becoming a reserve currency than existed two or three years ago, along with a belief that it should proceed on a gradual basis.

As to the propriety of the United States urging Japan to remove restrictions on its capital markets, he argued that such comments followed from the need, in an interdependent world, to avoid incompatible monetary policies. Why should rules in the capital markets of any country be beyond criticism when they could have major international effects?

On the exchange rate effects of internationalizing the yen, Solomon thought they could go either way. Internationalization of the dollar did not prevent periods of weakness; internationalization of the yen was not necessarily a prescription for its strength. Many factors underlie exchange rate movements. Because of these underlying factors, the international role of a currency could accentuate the trend of its movement toward strength or weakness.

MacLaury thought that there were different meanings attached to the concept of the internationalization of the yen. If by internationalization is meant open capital markets and open capital flows, then either appreciation or depreciation can result, depending on the net effect on capital flows. If the focus is on the development of a reserve currency status, then during the period in which there is a buildup of foreign balances denominated in yen, this capital inflow should lead to appreciation of the yen.

Bergsten, referring to McKinnon's proposal to improve the international monetary mechanisms, asked Solomon two questions: (1) Was it desirable to factor in the international demand for a currency in determining domestic monetary policy? To do so seemed to be consistent with the concern Solomon had expressed that capital movements for safe-haven purposes could swamp economic factors; and (2) Was it feasible to do so? In view of the fact that the Federal Reserve had to wrestle with huge structural changes in the money supply over the past year, such as money market accounts and the like, would it be any more difficult to take into account a sharp increase in foreign demand for the dollar?

Solomon replied that he was in favor of taking into account what was happening in exchange markets in formulating domestic monetary policy. McKinnon's proposal for coordinating the money supply of the United States, Japan, and Germany, quite apart from offsetting capital flows moving for political safe-haven reasons, was a very different matter. First, he thought it was an illusion to believe that a clear enough definition of the money supply existed to do that kind of fine tuning, all the more so because it would require coordinated action by several countries rather than the United States alone.

Second, to pump up the money supply now in order to bring the dollar rate down would ignore other important factors—notably the unfortunate effect it would have on inflationary expectations and on long-term interest rates. Thus he believed that there were technical, practical, and substantive difficulties with McKinnon's proposal.

Bergsten agreed that it would be difficult to increase the money supply sharply because of a sudden shift in policy to take into account the foreign demand for the dollar. But McKinnon is proposing a more gradual change in which markets and the public are educated to understand that the Federal Reserve will be taking the external factor into account in determining its monetary targets. Then, when such adjustments are made, it would be regarded as a normal part of the process.

Solomon said it might simply be a matter of degree. It comes down to where the line is drawn between his position that we ought to be looking at the exchange markets for what they tell us about the general question of tightness or ease in monetary policy and a sweeping solution in which the international factor would weigh very heavily. He would give it less weight.

McKinnon agreed with Solomon's point that a sudden increase in the money supply, without announcing a rationale, would exacerbate inflationary expectations. The financial markets have been captured by Milton Friedman, and people do look mainly at the monetary aggregates as the best measure of what the Federal Reserve is likely to do in the future. Therefore, his suggestion to use the exchange rate as a monetary indicator has to be announced in advance. The Federal Reserve would explain that it would permit an extraordinary expansion of the money supply as long as the dollar remained unduly appreciated, and then it would desist and, if necessary, go to negative money growth, if the dollar were to fall precipitately. This would then take care of the longer-term inflationary expectations problem.

Solomon insisted that even with a complete explanation of this rationale, it simply wouldn't work in the financial markets. Financial markets would see such a move as laying the basis for a subsequent surge in inflation. As a practical matter, therefore, such a policy would have unfortunate spillover effects.

Isiah Frank of the Johns Hopkins University commented on the importance of the U.S. budget deficit in this connection. Easing of monetary policy would be feasible if some progress were made on reducing the deficit, but with the deficit amounting to 5 percent of GNP and net private savings at 7 percent, any effort to deal with the exchange rate by easing monetary policy would be impractical.

George Eads of the University of Maryland asked whether

Solomon, in discussing possible intervention in exchange markets, was contemplating moving away from floating rates.

Solomon replied that he did not have in mind target zones or other ambitious proposals to manage rates. His reference was to concerted intervention when there was a consensus among the monetary authorities that an exchange rate had gotten out of line. The objective would be to correct the direction of change in line with the agreed consensus on the underlying fundamentals. This type of cooperative intervention can be useful as a signal to the foreign exchange markets. It can make a modest contribution to reducing the amplitude of swings in rates.

Emergency situations can arise, however, where markets are responding to strong bandwagon effects, divorced almost from the fundamentals, as in October–November 1978. Then, a massive intervention to produce a shock effect could be justified. In that event, some major domestic monetary measures are required, as well as intervention.

Eads asked Solomon what mechanism would be available to respond to a continuous appreciation from safe-haven effects.

Solomon said that in theory controls on capital inflows could be imposed. That would be undesirable, and every effort would be made to avoid it. However, if the crisis consisted of governments falling and capital flowing to the United States from many countries, there would be little left to do beyond massive intervention and controls. Needless to say, nothing on the horizon suggested a world crisis on this scale.

A participant asked Matsukawa: in view of the fact that interest rates in Japan were about one-third lower than in the United States, what prevented the development of a substantial Euroyen market to take advantage of this disparity?

Matsukawa responded that here again the monetary authorities were concerned that a well-developed Euroyen market would cause the Bank of Japan to lose control over the money supply. Nonetheless, in line with his earlier view about the stance of the monetary authorities, he noted that there were no prohibitions at present on floating yen bonds outside Japan. He estimated that outstanding yen-denominated assets outside Japan amounted to the equivalent of $100 billion, of which $30 billion is in the form of so-called Euroyen.

Overview

An Economic Summary

HENRY D. OWEN

THIS CONFERENCE had its origin in the "wise men's" report on Japan–U.S. economic relations presented to the president of the United States and the prime minister of Japan in January 1981.[1] One of the conclusions in that report is that "because savings in Japan are likely to remain relatively high compared to domestic investment demand, it is likely that Japan will have a long run tendency to run a current account surplus and be a capital exporter."[2] Examining this conclusion provides an opportunity to consider the interaction between trade and financial issues in economic relations between the two countries. Is Japan, in fact, likely to have a chronic current-account surplus? Will this surplus grow? Are present Japanese financial policies and institutions adequate to the management of this surplus? Will the surplus mean intensified trade problems with the United States? And is it a boon or a burden for the international economic system?

Framework

Yoshitomi began with an essay on fundamental points. Postwar Japan has gradually moved from being an international borrower to being an international creditor. This development can be explained by the relative decline in domestic demand for investment since 1974 while savings rates remained mainly unchanged. Although large government deficits have absorbed most of this excess in private-sector savings, some has in effect spilled over into a current-account surplus and therefore into the export of capital abroad.

For some years to come Japan is likely to continue to have a surplus in its trade in goods and services and thus to be a lender and investor abroad—in other words, an international creditor. The special circumstances of the post–oil shock period—when the absolute volume of Japan's goods exports rose strongly to pay for greatly increased costs of its oil imports—should not be

1. "Report of the Japan-United States Economic Relations Group," January 1981, available from National Technical Information Service, Springfield, Va. (doc. no. 11281–134801).

2. Ibid., p. vi.

considered the usual case. Normally, economic growth in Japan is not export-led; rather, Japan's surplus of exports over imports has been, and is likely to be, a rather stable proportion of GNP. In other words, the prospect is that Japan is close to becoming a mature international creditor, with its excess of domestic savings being transferred to capital-short countries and regions in the fashion prescribed by economics textbooks. Yoshitomi recognized, however, that Japan's capital markets need to be further liberalized to allow these transfers to be made with optimum efficiency.

McKinnon focused on monetary policy as a major cause of current difficulties. He estimated that the dollar was overvalued by 15 to 20 percent against the yen, a misalignment that has persisted since 1981. As a consequence, international competitive positions are distorted, trade problems exacerbated, some sectors of U.S. industry seriously handicapped, and protectionist pressures intensified.

This misalignment is the result of the failure of U.S. monetary authorities to allow for the large increase in foreign demand for dollar assets because of high interest rates in the United States and the use of the dollar as a safe-haven currency. To correct the problem, McKinnon argued for a sharp monetary expansion in the United States relative to monetary policy in Japan (and Germany). He also stressed the need for fiscal contraction in the United States. As interest rates fell in the United States and rose in Japan (and Germany), equilibrium in exchange markets would be restored. Trade problems would then be substantially eased and surplus Japanese savings would be available to finance development in the third world.

As a general matter, McKinnon stressed the need for coordinating monetary policies among the United States, Japan, and Germany, as the three leading market economies, in order to facilitate stable world economic growth. In response, Solomon said he believed U.S. monetary authorities should take exchange rate developments into account but was skeptical about the feasibility of coordinated international efforts to regulate the money supply, given the difficulties of defining the money supply in even one country.

Trade

Turning to trade, the discussion took a more conventional form. Senator Danforth said that Japan's large bilateral trade surplus with the United States was at bottom a political problem because it threatened American jobs. This should not be surprising to the

Japanese, because their farmers took exactly the same position in protesting against increasing imports of lower-cost agricultural products. His constituents in the automobile industry want to regain or keep their jobs, not to be trained for other work elsewhere in the country.

As a politician, he could not effectively address these concerns by asserting that protectionism would be bad for the country. Nor, unfortunately, could he point to equal treatment in Japan for American exports or argue that as many jobs were created in the export industries as were lost through import competition. For these reasons, he is seeking through reciprocity legislation to avoid protectionism by giving U.S. negotiators a more effective instrument to reduce barriers in other countries against U.S. exports.

Kobayashi responded that recent criticism of Japan's trade policies has been dominated by exaggeration and extremism. Japan's tariffs are among the lowest in the world. Nontariff barriers do indeed exist but they are being steadily removed. Japan can do more to free up its imports, particularly in the agricultural and service sectors. He argued, however, that the main need now is for greater initiative by American business to exploit a much more widely open Japanese market.

As to industrial policy and targeting, Kobayashi said that American concerns seemed to be misplaced. MITI's forecasts and goals for Japanese industry have some influence, mainly because of a tendency toward conformism among Japanese firms, but not because MITI has authority to impose its views. Whether all this has been of advantage to Japan's trade position is unclear. In respect to government subsidies for high technology, the aggregate figures show that government's share of spending for research and development is larger in the United States than it is in Japan.

Niskanen tended to discount both the trade and exchange rate issues as legitimate grounds for rifts between Japan and the United States. He viewed the large U.S. bilateral trade deficit with Japan as being of the same character as the large U.S. trade surplus with Western Europe: there were sound economic reasons for both.

The appreciation of the dollar in relation to the yen had certainly put U.S. business at a disadvantage, but the main source of that difficulty was in the United States, not Japan. Large existing and prospective U.S. budget deficits contributed to high U.S. interest rates, which in turn attracted capital from abroad and drove up the price of the dollar.

In Niskanen's view, the real problems were all issues that could be resolved in the mutual interest. Relaxation of Japanese restraints on imports of agricultural products and services is an example. Further liberalization of Japan's capital market is another. Action on both issues, he noted, would further weaken the yen and thus be to the short-run trade disadvantage of the United States. Over the longer term, the efficiency gains would benefit both countries, as well as the rest of the world.

Actions related to the common defense are a third problem area. Despite agreement on goals and a commonality of interests, differences continue to exist on rules for exporting strategic technology and on sharing the costs of the common defense.

On the other hand, Niskanen was less concerned about the effect of Japan's industrial policy on trade. As a general matter, he saw no need for national economic policies and practices among countries to be the same or similar for trade to take place. The main requirement is that foreign firms be accorded national treatment in conducting business in other countries.

Financial issues

Financial issues, as the counterpart to trade flows, then came up for discussion. Matsukawa stressed that despite widespread American perceptions to the contrary, Japan had not kept the yen cheap to strengthen its competitive position. The yen rate in 1981–82 was heavily influenced by the large and growing capital outflow from Japan. This outflow resulted from: (1) actions taken at the beginning of 1981 to liberalize Japan's capital markets, and (2) lower interest rates in Japan compared to those in the United States. He thought that the size of this net capital outflow had become abnormally large and would not be sustained in the future; as it declined, pressure on the yen would be lifted.

Matsukawa acknowledged that while the secondary bond market in Japan was free from controls, residual restraints existed on primary bond issues because the government desired strongly to reduce the financial cost of the large volume of national bond issues. He also said that Japanese monetary authorities do not welcome the internationalization of the yen, mainly because it would weaken their ability to control the money supply. Nonetheless, Matsukawa prophesied that these restraints will continue to be weakened and that the yen will be used increasingly as a reserve asset because such developments are natural economic and monetary steps in global development.

Solomon's comments on the relationship between trade and financial problems took a different direction. The Japanese obviously had the right to indulge their preference for a high savings rate. Nor did he see why Japan's current-account surplus need be disruptively large. Problems arose, in his view, because Japan maintained restrictions in domestic financial markets and institutions that tended to restrain consumption and artificially push up the saving rate. Continuance of these restraints on consumer spending was in contradiction with Japan's liberalization of its international capital market; in combination, these two policies caused savings to be abnormally high and to be transferred abroad via the current-account surplus, which put pressure on the international system.

He also suggested that Japan's chronic deficit in its services account was likely to decline because of the narrowing of its transport deficit and the growing reverse flow of income from investments and royalties from licensing technology. To that extent, there would be less need in the future for an offsetting surplus in the trade account.

Generally, Solomon questioned whether the trade and financial problems under discussion were specific to Japan or were not more accurately a reflection of a worldwide problem. In any given year, a very large Japanese current-account surplus could pose problems. But what makes such surpluses worse, whether in Japan or any other country, is the fact that they can be exaggerated by changes in exchange rates dominated by capital flows for safe-haven purposes. These flows can distort the exchange rate as a price governing the movement of tradable goods. If serious enough, such distortions might justify offsetting government intervention.

Conclusions

Running through these presentations and the discussions following them were two general themes. First, Japan's current-account surplus is not a passing phenomenon but a more long-lasting consequence of Japan's unusually high rate of domestic savings and its growing affluence. Under normal circumstances, this surplus would be likely to constitute a fairly constant percentage of GNP, not a rising one. There is no reason for other countries to resent this development, but there is reason for Japan to make it more productive for the rest of the world by developing more effective policies and institutions governing capital exports—that is, lending abroad, foreign direct investment, and aid to the third world. Both the industrial and developing worlds need more capital to finance necessary investment. Japan's high savings rate makes it inevitable that Japan will play an important role in meeting this need.

Second, Japan-U.S. economic tensions are to some degree the result of special transitory circumstances rather than the product of long-term forces that will be difficult to alter. These circumstances include the dislocation following the two oil price shocks; differences between the policies chosen by the United States and by other industrial countries in the fight against inflation; the selective, gradual dismantling of economic controls in Japan; and the large volume of safe-haven capital flows that have been affecting exchange rates. The impact of these disturbances will diminish somewhat as the world economy completes the process of wringing out inflation and regaining satisfactory economic growth. As this happens, the exchange rate will again become a strong equilibrating force governing the movement of goods and services. And Japan's savings will be seen as a potentially strong force to promote world development.

In the meanwhile, patience and good sense will be necessary in both countries to avoid actions regarding Japan's current-account surplus that would be economically costly and, in the end, politically dangerous.

Political Dimensions

NOBUHIKO USHIBA

THROUGH MY STAY in Washington as ambassador and frequent visits as a government negotiator and then as a private citizen, I have witnessed and at times participated in mutual efforts to bring the United States and Japan closer together as partners and allies. It is in Washington through friendship with many individuals that I have developed a profound respect for the United States for its leadership in the advancement of the free world and the open world trade and monetary systems.

On returning this time, however, I find in Washington a mood that I have never encountered before. I had been reading and hearing about the present atmosphere in Washington back in Tokyo, but frankly since my arrival here I have been shocked and dismayed by its intensity and particularly by the resentment expressed against Japan. I believe that I am accustomed to highly political statements in the political capital of this great nation, and yet some of the pronouncements by the leaders of the government, Congress, business, and labor that I came across in the past few days go far beyond anything I ever heard in my long association with the United States.

I would like to speak briefly on the political dimensions of the bilateral economic relationship. My comments will be very frank, befitting a talk between old friends. One obvious conclusion I draw from the discussion in today's symposium is that there are no sweeping policy measures readily available in either country to put an end once and for all to the economic tensions we have been facing. Perhaps the best we can do, at least in the short run, is to muddle through this period of continuing tension. It is, then, all the more important for both countries to manage the political relationship so as to avoid extreme politicization of these economic tensions. Failure to do so could jeopardize the constructive cooperation so important to both countries. The discussion at this conference, which has been carried out in a dispassionate and analytical manner, has certainly been encouraging to me personally. But a question raised in my own mind is how representative this group is of attitudes in the United States generally or for that matter in Washington.

Criticism of Japan

What is most worrisome to those of us deeply committed to our relationship is that the unbridled criticism of Japan taking place here over the past year or so is creating a growing irritation and resentment among many Japanese. They see themselves as the target of unjust and irrational American criticism that places Japan in the role of scapegoat. In response to these unending American pressures, an increasingly ominous chauvinistic tone is emerging in Japan. Many Japanese, including government and political leaders, now bitterly complain that the United States is putting the blame on Japan for problems basically of its own making. They are demanding to know why Japanese have to be penalized for working hard and be called unfair just because they have been successful. There is a danger that this growing resentment among Japanese will in turn aggravate American reactions and lead to a tragic downward spiral of mutual recrimination.

A large number of Japanese are becoming deeply agitated by speeches and statements by high-ranking U.S. government officials and congressional leaders who denounce Japan on charges that Japanese consider to be unsubstantiated or totally false. It is hard for most Japanese to believe, for example, that any significant amount of export subsidies or other incentives are presently provided in Japan, as charged by some Americans. In recent months, Japanese suddenly started hearing a chorus of condemnation by Americans of Japan's industrial policy and industrial targeting. What puzzles Japanese is that, on the one hand, the United States seems to be trying to emulate the Japanese experience and, on the other hand, is condemning it as unfair.

What is further troubling to Japanese is that they are not clear as to what is meant by Japan's "industrial policy" that Americans criticize. Many Japanese tend to believe that this ambiguous term, which is without solid substantiation, is conveniently used as a cover for the adoption of protectionist measures. These Japanese are incredulous when they hear arguments used by some responsible American leaders that Japan should be penalized for its so-called industrial policy in the past, when Japan was not a member of the OECD and still was considered to be a developing country. (They wonder what might be the implications of such an attitude for the nations seeking industrialization or on the verge of industrialization.) Through these recriminations, most unfortunately, the United States is beginning to project the image of a defeatist, selfish, and self-righteous nation among a surprisingly large number of Japanese.

I caution such countrymen of mine not to overreact to the present situation and remind them that it is not all of the United States that has undergone such a change. I know many American friends who hold on to their traditional competitive spirit and work ethic and who are dedicated to a free and open international economy. I know also many who remain deeply committed to a harmonious bilateral relationship with Japan.

In this connection it was particularly gratifying to hear President Reagan in his February 22, 1983, speech before the American Legion state that "the U.S.-Japanese relationship remains the centerpiece of our Asian policy" and to reaffirm, as we in Japan believe, that "together, the United States and Japan can make an enormous contribution to the economic dynamism and technological progress needed for economic growth and development throughout the world." This was a most important statement, which I believe places the U.S.-Japan relationship in its proper perspective. It is essential that the president's broad and positive approach not be undermined by the chorus of voices at lower levels of the administration that seem to describe the relationship in adversarial rather than cooperative terms.

Managing the relationship

I am deeply troubled by the prospect that this growing emotional and acrimonious interaction between the United States and Japan, if left alone, could jeopardize the basic foundations of the relationship that we have been building up over so many years. Both countries should have a clear recognition that there is too much at stake to let our relationship deteriorate through irresponsible actions and statements designed for domestic political consumption and short-term gains. As the largest and the second largest industrial democracies, we have shared interests in the international economic and political order. We also have an important and mutually beneficial relationship in the economic, security, and cultural fields. It is vital that we put the contentious economic issues between us in the broad perspective of the president's statement and address them jointly in a reasoned and constructive manner.

Another point to be made is that the unfortunate atmosphere created largely by this "bashing of Japan" is making it very difficult for those in Japan committed to the bilateral relationship, including Prime Minister Yasuhiro Nakasone, to pursue policies and programs that are designed to promote greater cooperation between us. Japanese certainly should not be oblivious to our obligation to assume a larger role in the international community, commensurate with Japan's economic power. However, an acrimonious atmosphere in relations with our major ally is hindering the emergence of a national consensus to expand cooperation in economic affairs, security, development assistance, and other matters.

Indeed, there is a wide and bright horizon of opportunities and urgent needs for our two countries to join forces and make cooperative contributions to the international community. This troubled world more than ever needs American prestige and leadership, not only as a preserver of peace and stability but as a champion of an open international economic system based on rules and agreements. It is with such a United States that Japan can most readily and willingly work. It bears repeated emphasis that Japan's constructive contribution to the international community will be found not in unilateral actions but in the context of an alliance relationship with the United States.

While frictions between the United States and Japan are inevitable, particularly in their economic relations, it is essential that these frictions be managed so they do not obscure the overriding importance of our common interests or prevent constructive cooperation in bringing about the kind of international order in which both societies thrive. I am sure the kind of joint analysis and constructive discussion that has taken place at this conference will contribute to this end and I hope a continuation of this effort will be possible in the future.

Conference Participants

C. Michael Aho
Economist, Office of Senator Bill Bradley

J. W. Anderson
Editorial Writer, The Washington Post

Ronald Aqua
Program Director, United States-Japan Foundation

Joji Arai
Director, Japan Productivity Center

Ichiro Araki
President, Marubeni America Corporation

Thomas R. Atkinson
Vice-President, General Motors Overseas Corporation

William F. Averyt
Vice-President, International Business-Government Counsellors, Inc.

Max Baucus
Member of U.S. Senate

C. Fred Bergsten
Director, Institute for International Economics

Michael Blaker
Director, Japanese Studies, Center for Strategic and International Studies, Georgetown University

I. M. Booth
Executive Vice-President and Chief Operating Officer, Polaroid Corporation

Thornton F. Bradshaw
Chairman of the Board and Chief Executive Officer, RCA Corporation

Richard Brandon
Minority Staff Director, Senate Budget Committee

John G. Brim
Vice-President, Salomon Brothers Inc.

John F. Burlingame
Vice-Chairman, General Electric Company

James B. Burnham
U.S. Executive Director, The World Bank

Jack B. Button
*Former Executive Director,
The Japan-United States Economic Relations Group*

George N. Caruby
U.S. Representative and Manager, International Business Information, Inc.

Pat Choate
TRW, Inc.

William R. Cline
Senior Fellow, Institute for International Economics

James L. Cochrane
Deputy Director, East Asian Analysis, Central Intelligence Agency

A. E. Cohen
Senior Vice-President, Merck & Co., Inc.
President, Merck Sharp and Dohme International

Dan Cordtz
Economics Editor, ABC News

John C. Danforth
Member of U.S. Senate

Masato Degawa
Guest Scholar, The Brookings Institution

Donald E. deKieffer
Principal, Plaia, Schaumberg and deKieffer

Joly Dixon
First Secretary,
Economic Delegation of the Commission of the European Communities

Angier Biddle Duke
Chairman, United States-Japan Foundation

George Eads
Professor, School of Public Affairs, University of Maryland

Henry H. Fowler
Chairman, Goldman Sachs International Corporation

Lawrence A. Fox
Vice-President for International Affairs,
National Association of Manufacturers

Isaiah Frank
Professor of International Economics, The Johns Hopkins University

Orville L. Freeman
President and Chief Executive Officer, Business International Corporation

Edward R. Fried
Senior Fellow, The Brookings Institution

Hiroshi Fukuda
Counselor, Embassy of Japan

Kiyohiko Fukushima
Nomura Research Institute, New York

Sam M. Gibbons
Member of U.S. House of Representatives

Ruth S. Gold
Special Assistant to the Assistant Secretary for Economic and Business Affairs,
Department of State

Stephen Gomersall
First Secretary, Embassy of Great Britain

Kent Hance
Member of U.S. House of Representatives

Yasushi Hara
American Bureau Chief, The Asahi Shimbun

Yutaka Harada
International Cooperation Department,
National Institute for Research Advancement

Cecil Heftel
Member of U.S. House of Representatives

Richard W. Heimlich
Director, U.S.-Japanese Trade Relations and Strategies, Motorola Inc.

Robert Herzstein
Senior Partner, Arnold and Porter

Norman M. Hinerfeld
Chairman of the Executive Committee, Kayser-Roth Corporation

Atsuo Hirano
General Manager, The Mitsubishi Bank, Ltd.

Robert C. Holland
President, Committee for Economic Development

Robert D. Hormats
Vice-President, Goldman, Sachs and Co.

Herbert Hubben
Vice-President–International, Eaton Corporation

Gary Hufbauer
Senior Fellow, Institute for International Economics

Robert S. Ingersoll
Chairman, Japan Society, Inc.
Former U.S. Ambassador to Japan

U. Alexis Johnson
President, Japan-American Society of Washington
Former U.S. Ambassador to Japan

James R. Jones
Member of U.S. House of Representatives

Julius L. Katz
Chairman of the Board, ACLI International Commodity Services, Inc.

Hanazuka Kazuya
Investor and Press Relations, Hitachi America, Ltd.

Anne G. Keatley
Project Director, Office of International Affairs,
National Academy of Sciences

Theodore F. Killheffer
Senior International Counsel, Legal Department,
E. I. du Pont de Nemours and Company, Inc.

Norman Klath
Vice-President, Morgan Guaranty Trust Company

Arthur Klauser
Senior Vice-President, Mitsui and Company Ltd.

Yotaro Kobayashi
President, Fuji-Xerox Co., Ltd.

Shinzo Kobori
Senior Vice-President, C. Itoh and Company (America), Inc.

Keiichi Koda
Assistant Professor, Department of Economics,
Virginia Polytechnic Institute and State University

Richard T. Koskella
Analyst for International Affairs and National Security,
U.S. Senate Budget Committee

Michihiko Kunihiro
Minister, Embassy of Japan

Naotada Kurakake
Executive Vice-President, National Institute for Research Advancement

Denis Lamb
Deputy Assistant Secretary for Trade and Commercial Affairs,
Department of State

Steven Lande
Manchester Associates

Eugene K. Lawson
Deputy Assistant Secretary of Commerce for East Asia and the Pacific,
Department of Commerce

James J. Lenehan
Vice-President, Rockwell International Overseas Corporation

Lehmann Li
Policy Analyst, Office of Policy Development, The White House

Rochelle Lipsitz
Business Intelligence, Sears World Trade, Inc.

David MacEachron
President, Japan Society, Inc.

Ronald I. McKinnon
Professor of Economics, Stanford University,
Visiting Scholar, Hoover Institution

Bruce K. MacLaury
President, The Brookings Institution

Robert McLellan
Vice-President, Government Affairs, FMC Corporation

Robert H. Marik
Vice-President, Public Affairs, Merck Sharp and Dohme International

R. L. Martino
Vice-President and Treasurer, American Cyanamid Company

Mike M. Masaoka
President, Mike Masaoka Associates

Michiya Matsukawa
Chairman, The Nikko Research Center, Ltd.
Former Japanese Vice-Minister of Finance

Fumio Matsuo
Bureau Chief, Kyodo News Service

P. Reed Maurer
Vice-President–Japan and China, Merck Sharp and Dohme International

Michio Mizoguchi
Minister Plenipotentiary, Embassy of Japan

John V. Moller
Vice-President, Manchester Associates, Ltd.

Ronald A. Morse
Secretary, East Asian Program, The Wilson Center,
The Smithsonian Institution

Yoshio Nakamura
Visiting Economist, Japan Economic Institute of America

Dick K. Nanto
Head, Industry Analysis and Finance Section,
Congressional Research Service, Library of Congress

Kimi Narita
Vice-President and Senior Economist, Bank of America

William A. Niskanen
Member, Council of Economic Advisers, Executive Office of the President

Clovis F. Obermesser
President, Asia Pacific, Westinghouse Electric Corporation

Yoshio Okawara
Ambassador of Japan, Embassy of Japan

Hideaki Otaka
Senior Executive Coordinator, Toyota Motor Sales, U.S.A. Inc.

Henry D. Owen
Former Ambassador-at-Large and Special Representative of President Carter
for Economic Summits

George R. Packard
Dean, School of Advanced International Studies,
The Johns Hopkins University

Hugh T. Patrick
Professor of Economics, Yale Economic Growth Center, Yale University

Robert B. Peabody
President, American Iron and Steel Institute

Charles S. Pearson
Professor of International Economics, The Johns Hopkins University

Robert A. Perkins
Vice-President–Washington Office–Public Affairs, Chrysler Corporation

Richard W. Petree
President, United States–Japan Foundation

Lino J. Piedra
International Liaison–Manager, Chrysler Corporation

Rolf Piekarz
Group Leader, Socioeconomic Effects of Science and Technology,
Policy Research and Analysis, National Science Foundation

C. Tait Ratcliffe
President, International Business Information, Inc.

James K. Reed
Manager, Long-Range Planning, Union Pacific Corporation

Alfred Reifman
Senior Specialist in International Economics,
Congressional Research Service, Library of Congress

F. Michael P. Riding
Senior Vice-President, Chemical Bank

Richard R. Rivers
Partner, Akin, Gump, Strauss, Hauer and Feld

Roger W. Robinson
Senior Staff Member, National Security Council,
Executive Office of the President

William V. Roth, Jr
Member of U.S. Senate

Gary Saxonhouse
Professor of Economics, University of Michigan

J. Robert Schaetzel
Director, Honeywell Inc.
Former U.S. Ambassador to the European Communities

Frank W. Schiff
Vice-President and Chief Economist, Committee for Economic Development

Susan C. Schwab
Legislative Assistant, Office of Senator John C. Danforth

Robert S. Seal
Director, International Affairs, The Boeing Company

Albert L. Seligmann
Director, Office of Japanese Affairs, East Asian and Pacific Affairs,
Department of State

Philippe Selz
Counselor, Embassy of France

Sen-Ichi Shamoto
Senior Vice-President, Nissho Iwai American Corporation

Arthur V. Smyth
Vice-President, Weyerhaeuser Company

Anthony M. Solomon
President, Federal Reserve Bank of New York

Don K. Spencer
Executive Vice-President, Pecten Chemicals, Shell Oil Company

Elmer B. Staats
Former Comptroller General of the United States

Timothy W. Stanley
President, International Economic Studies Institute

Sydney Stein, Jr.
Honorary Trustee, The Brookings Institution

Paula Stern
Commissioner, U.S. International Trade Commission

Robert S. Strauss
Partner, Akin, Gump, Strauss, Hauer and Feld

Yasuhiko Suzuki
Vice-President, Nissan Motor Corporation in U.S.A.

T. Takahara
Managing Director, C. Itoh and Company (Japan), Ltd.

William E. Timmons
President, Timmons and Company

Seiichi Toshida
Counselor, Embassy of Japan

Philip H. Trezise
Senior Fellow, The Brookings Institution

Nobuyuki Ueda
Deputy Manager and Economist, The Long-Term Credit Bank of Japan

Masayasu Ueno
Joint General Manager, The Sumitomo Bank, Ltd.

Nobuhiko Ushiba
Former Ambassador of Japan to the United States

Frank A. Weil
Senior Partner, Ginsburg, Feldman, Weil and Bress

Donald B. Westmore
Member, Policy Planning Staff, Department of State

Alan William Wolff
Partner, Verner, Liipfert, Bernard and McPherson

Shigenobu Yoshida
*Director, International Cooperation Department,
National Institute for Research Advancement*

Bunroku Yoshino
Adviser, Keidanren

Masaru Yoshitomi
Chief Economist, Economic Research Institute, Economic Planning Agency